Lessons from Selected Program and Policy Areas

Howard S. Bloom, *Editor*
New York University

David S. Cordray, *Editor*
U.S. General Accounting Office

Richard J. Light, *Editor*
Harvard University

NEW DIRECTIONS FOR PROGRAM EVALUATION
A Publication of the American Evaluation Association
A joint organization of the Evaluation Research Society and the Evaluation Network
MARK W. LIPSEY, *Editor-in-Chief*
Claremont Graduate School

Number 37, Spring 1988

Paperback sourcebooks in
The Jossey-Bass Higher Education and
Social and Behavioral Sciences Series

Jossey-Bass Inc., Publishers
San Francisco • London

Howard S. Bloom, David S. Cordray, Richard J. Light (eds.).
Lessons from Selected Program and Policy Areas.
New Directions for Program Evaluation, no. 37.
San Francisco: Jossey-Bass, 1988.

New Directions for Program Evaluation Series
A publication of the American Evaluation Association
Mark W. Lipsey, *Editor-in-Chief*

Copyright © 1988 by Jossey-Bass Inc., Publishers
and
Jossey-Bass Limited

Copyright under International, Pan American, and Universal Copyright Conventions. All rights reserved. No part of this issue may be reproduced in any form—except for brief quotation (not to exceed 500 words) in a review or professional work—without permission in writing from the publishers.

New Directions for Program Evaluation is published quarterly by Jossey-Bass Inc., Publishers (publication number USPS 449-050), and is sponsored by the American Evaluation Association. Second-class postage rates are paid at San Francisco, California, and at additional mailing offices. POSTMASTER: Send address changes to Jossey-Bass Inc., Publishers, 350 Sansome Street, San Francisco, California 94104.

Editorial correspondence should be sent to the Editor-in-Chief, Mark Lipsey, Psychology Department, Claremont Graduate School, Claremont, Calif. 91711.

Library of Congress Catalog Card Number LC 85-644749
International Standard Serial Number ISSN 0164-7989
International Standard Book Number ISBN 1-55542-924-6

Cover art by WILLI BAUM
Manufactured in the United States of America

Ordering Information

The paperback sourcebooks listed below are published quarterly and can be ordered either by subscription or single copy.

Subscriptions cost $52.00 per year for institutions, agencies, and libraries. Individuals can subscribe at the special rate of $39.00 per year *if payment is by personal check*. (Note that the full rate of $52.00 applies if payment is by institutional check, even if the subscription is designated for an individual.) Standing orders are accepted.

Single copies are available at $12.95 when payment accompanies order. (California, New Jersey, New York, and Washington, D.C., residents please include appropriate sales tax.) For billed orders, cost per copy is $12.95 plus postage and handling.

Substantial discounts are offered to organizations and individuals wishing to purchase bulk quantities of Jossey-Bass sourcebooks. Please inquire.

Please note that these prices are for the academic year 1987–88 and are subject to change without prior notice. Also, some titles may be out of print and therefore not available for sale.

To ensure correct and prompt delivery, all orders must give either the *name of an individual* or an *official purchase order number*. Please submit your order as follows:

Subscriptions: specify series and year subscription is to begin.
Single Copies: specify sourcebook code (such as, PE1) and first two words of title.

Mail orders for United States and Possessions, Latin America, Canada, Japan, Australia, and New Zealand to:
   Jossey-Bass Inc., Publishers
   350 Sansome Street
   San Francisco, California 94104

Mail orders for all other parts of the world to:
   Jossey-Bass Limited
   28 Banner Street
   London EC1Y 8QE

New Directions for Program Evaluation Series
Mark W. Lipsey, *Editor-in-Chief*

PE1 *Exploring Purposes and Dimensions,* Scarvia B. Anderson, Claire D. Coles
PE2 *Evaluating Federally Sponsored Programs,* Charlotte C. Rentz, R. Robert Rentz
PE3 *Monitoring Ongoing Programs,* Donald L. Grant

PE4 *Secondary Analysis*, Robert F. Boruch
PE5 *Utilization of Evaluative Information*, Larry A. Braskamp, Robert D. Brown
PE6 *Measuring the Hard-to-Measure*, Edward H. Loveland
PE7 *Values, Ethics, and Standards in Evaluation*, Robert Perloff, Evelyn Perloff
PE8 *Training Program Evaluators*, Lee Sechrest
PE9 *Assessing and Interpreting Outcomes*, Samuel Ball
PE10 *Evaluation of Complex Systems*, Ronald J. Wooldridge
PE11 *Measuring Effectiveness*, Dan Baugher
PE12 *Federal Efforts to Develop New Evaluation Methods*, Nick L. Smith
PE13 *Field Assessments of Innovative Evaluation Methods*, Nick L. Smith
PE14 *Making Evaluation Research Useful to Congress*, Leonard Saxe, Daniel Koretz
PE15 *Standards for Evaluation Practice*, Peter H. Rossi
PE16 *Applications of Time Series Analysis to Evaluation*, Garlie A. Forehand
PE17 *Stakeholder-Based Evaluation*, Anthony S. Bryk
PE18 *Management and Organization of Program Evaluation*, Robert G. St. Pierre
PE19 *Philosophy of Evaluation*, Ernest R. House
PE20 *Developing Effective Internal Evaluation*, Arnold J. Love
PE21 *Making Effective Use of Mailed Questionnaires*, Daniel C. Lockhart
PE22 *Secondary Analysis of Available Data Bases*, David J. Bowering
PE23 *Evaluating the New Information Technologies*, Jerome Johnston
PE24 *Issues in Data Synthesis*, William H. Yeaton, Paul M. Wortman
PE25 *Culture and Evaluation*, Michael Quinn Patton
PE26 *Economic Evaluations of Public Programs*, James S. Catterall
PE27 *Utilizing Prior Research in Evaluation Planning*, David S. Cordray
PE28 *Randomization and Field Experimentation*, Robert F. Boruch, Werner Wothke
PE29 *Teaching of Evaluation Across the Disciplines*, Barbara Gross Davis
PE30 *Naturalistic Evaluation*, David D. Williams
PE31 *Advances in Quasi-Experimental Design and Analysis*, William M. K. Trochim
PE32 *Measuring Efficiency: An Assessment of Data Envelopment Analysis*, Richard H. Silkman
PE33 *Using Program Theory in Evaluation*, Leonard Bickman
PE34 *Evaluation Practice in Review*, David S. Cordray, Howard S. Bloom, Richard J. Light
PE35 *Multiple Methods in Program Evaluation*, Melvin M. Mark, R. Lance Shotland
PE36 *The Client Perspective on Evaluation*, Jeri Nowakowski

Contents

Editors' Notes 1
Howard S. Bloom, David S. Cordray, Richard J. Light

1. Work-Welfare Programs 7
Judith M. Gueron
Although the effects of work-welfare program arrangements are small, they are often large enough to justify program costs.

2. Direct Cash Low-Income Housing Assistance 29
Stephen D. Kennedy
Effects of housing assistance are relatively small, except for those who are induced to change housing. For families who do not move, rent burden is reduced.

3. Examining Racial Discrimination with Fair Housing Audits 47
John Yinger
Housing discrimination is pervasive in many cities, affects many minority groups, and takes a variety of forms.

4. Juvenile Delinquency Intervention 63
Mark W. Lipsey
Contrary to early claims that "nothing works," cumulative evidence shows positive treatment effects of modest but not trivial magnitude.

5. Randomized Experiments in Criminal Sanctions 85
Lawrence W. Sherman
Conflicting findings from experiments in criminal sanctions can be better understood by examining characteristics of the sanctions, offenders, and offenses.

6. Mental Health Program Evaluation and Needs Assessment 99
James A. Ciarlo, Charles Windle
Changes in the sociopolitical context of the past decade point to the need for "echelon-specific" evaluations and more attention to both internal and external evaluation and replication.

Index 121

New Directions for Program Evaluation

A Quarterly Publication of the American Evaluation Association
(A Joint Organization of the Evaluation Research Society and the
Evaluation Network)

Editor-in-Chief:

Mark W. Lipsey, Psychology, Claremont Graduate School

Editorial Advisory Board:

Scarvia B. Anderson, Psychology, Georgia Institute of Technology
Gerald L. Barkdoll, U.S. Food and Drug Administration, Washington, D.C.
Robert F. Boruch, Psychology, Northwestern University
Timothy C. Brock, Psychology, Ohio State University
Donald T. Campbell, Social Relations, Lehigh University
Eleanor Chelimsky, U.S. General Accounting Office, Washington, D.C.
James A. Ciarlo, Mental Health Systems Evaluation, University of Denver
Ross F. Conner, Social Ecology, University of California, Irvine
William W. Cooley, Learning Research and Development Center, University of Pittsburgh
David S. Cordray, U.S. General Accounting Office, Washington, D.C.
Robert W. Covert, Evaluation Research Center, University of Virginia
Lois-Ellin Datta, U.S. General Accounting Office, Washington, D.C.
Barbara Gross Davis, Educational Development, University of California, Berkeley
Howard E. Freeman, Sociology, University of California, Los Angeles
Egon G. Guba, Education, Indiana University
Edward S. Halpern, AT&T Bell Laboratories, Naperville, Illinois
Harry P. Hatry, The Urban Institute, Washington, D.C.
Michael Hendricks, MH Associates, Washington, D.C.
Gary T. Henry, Joint Legislative Audit and Review Commission, Virginia
Dennis H. Holmes, Education, George Washington University
Ernest R. House, CIRCE, University of Illinois, Urbana-Champaign
Jeanette M. Jerrell, Cognos Associates, Los Altos, California
Karen E. Kirkhart, Social Work, Syracuse University
Henry M. Levin, Education, Stanford University
Richard J. Light, Government, Harvard University
Charles McClintock, Human Service Studies, Cornell University
William A. McConnell, San Francisco Community Mental Health Programs
Jeri Nowakowski, Leadership and Education Policy Studies, Northern Illinois University

Michael Q. Patton, International Programs, University of Minnesota
Charles S. Reichardt, Psychology, University of Denver
Leonard Rutman, Price Waterhouse Associates, Ottawa, Ontario
Thomas A. Schwandt, Center for Educational Development, University of Illinois, Chicago
Penny Sebring, NORC, University of Chicago
Lee Sechrest, Psychology, University of Arizona
Jana Kay Slater, California State Department of Education
Midge F. Smith, Agricultural and Extension Education, University of Maryland
Nick L. Smith, Education, Syracuse University
Robert E. Stake, CIRCE, University of Illinois, Urbana-Champaign
Robert M. Stonehill, U.S. Department of Education
Daniel L. Stufflebeam, Evaluation Center, Western Michigan University
Robert St. Pierre, Abt Associates, Inc., Cambridge, Massachusetts
Carol H. Weiss, Education, Harvard University
Joseph S. Wholey, School of Public Administration, University of Southern California
Paul M. Wortman, ISR, University of Michigan
William H. Yeaton, ISR, University of Michigan

American Evaluation Association, 9555 Persimmon Tree Road, Potomac, MD 20854

Editors' Notes

In 1986 the first annual meeting of the American Evaluation Association (AEA) was held in Kansas City, Missouri. As organizers for this meeting, we invited a variety of distinguished speakers to comment on past findings and future directions for program evaluation as a field. This is the second volume of *New Directions for Program Evaluation* that draws on papers invited for the 1986 AEA conference to explore what we have learned from past evaluations. Whereas the first volume (Cordray, Bloom, and Light, 1987) covered lessons on how to organize, design, and interpret evaluation studies, this issue focuses on substantive lessons from major evaluations across a broad array of topics. These topics include discussions of the effects of work-welfare programs, low-income housing assistance, juvenile delinquency interventions, and various criminal sanctions. Methods for detecting housing discrimination and progress in mental health evaluation and needs assessment are also described. Naturally, these topics do not represent all program and policy areas pertinent to program evaluation; nevertheless, the authors bring forward a broad range of experience and thereby provide insights that are likely to be widely generalizable.

In Chapter One, Judith M. Gueron describes what we have learned about reforming welfare through work. Evidence from a series of large-scale evaluations on state work-welfare initiatives shows that (1) it is feasible, under some conditions, to tie welfare receipt to job-training program participation; (2) a variety of program arrangements will yield effective treatments; (3) effects are greater for enrollees *without* recent work experience than for those with such experience; and (4) overall, the programs achieved relatively modest but important increases in employment (usually large enough to justify program cost), although this varied by state and target group. Gueron concludes that the results support the strongest claims of neither program advocates nor program critics. In closing, she identifies numerous unanswered questions that set an agenda for future research on this topic.

In Chapter Two, Stephen D. Kennedy uses findings from several major studies to demonstrate that direct cash housing assistance to low-income families is less expensive per dollar value of rental housing provided than is government-constructed public housing. Examination of program participation patterns and the effects of participation on housing condition reveals that households are much more likely to participate if their housing already meets program standards. For such participants, most of the assistance goes to reducing rent burdens. Yet changes in housing conditions for the poor are greatest for those who are induced to meet housing requirements (usually, by moving). Lastly, Kennedy indicates that use of the existing housing stock does not generally reach those in the worst housing. From this evidence, he concludes that more attention should be focused on (1) defining the target population for housing assistance; (2) clarifying the role of public housing in providing access to housing when private direct cash programs do not succeed (for example, when housing is in limited supply); (3) identifying ways of reducing public housing costs; and (4) promoting changes in public housing over time.

In Chapter Three, John Yinger examines measurement issues in housing discrimination. He summarizes the results of five major studies that used an innovative measure of discrimination, a quasi-experimental technique referred to as *fair housing audits*. This procedure assesses racial and ethnic discrimination exhibited by real estate brokers. Analyses based on this procedure reveal that the level of discrimination and probability of encountering it is very high in many cities; many groups (blacks, Hispanics, and Asians) are affected by a variety of forms of discrimination. Yinger argues that discrimination reflects economic incentives faced by real estate brokers who are concerned about maintaining their primarily white clientele, more so than individual broker prejudice per se.

In Chapter Four, Mark W. Lipsey takes a broad look at the evolution of research on the effects of juvenile delinquency interventions. He first describes how a combination of changing political forces (a shift in values from rehabilitation to retribution) and the accumulation of seemingly negative research findings produced a growing skepticism about juvenile delinquency interventions. Since the early 1980s, however, the quality of research evidence has improved and new methods have been applied that provide a different perspective on the effects of such interventions. Summarizing three meta-analyses of this research, Lipsey shows that the existing literature reveals positive treatment effects of modest, but not trivial magnitude. This review also shows that improvements in state-of-the-art evaluation methodology can be made. Lipsey identifies several promising avenues for making such improvements. These include more attention to treatment theory, targeting juveniles, program implementation, sensitive outcome assessments, statistical power, and the use of high-quality research designs.

In Chapter Five, Lawrence W. Sherman examines the conflicting findings surrounding various assessments of the effects of criminal sanctions. Available experimental evidence shows that sanctions increase, decrease, or have no effects on subsequent criminal behavior. He argues that to understand this body of research requires careful attention to variations in the sanctions that are tested and to the offenders and offenses that are involved. Sherman identifies several key features of sanctions—

their severity, certainty, and celerity (speed), and sanction by offender interactions—that seem to be associated with evidence on effectiveness. These results pave the way for more refined theorizing and empirical assessment in the future.

Finally, in Chapter Six, James A. Ciarlo and Charles Windle outline the evolution of mental health program evaluation produced by changes in nature of these programs and shifts in the roles of federal, state, and local governments. These changes have broadened our perspective on what constitutes useful information in mental health services research. This chapter paints a clear picture of the need for multiple approaches to answering questions from numerous echelons within the mental health system (such as internal and external evaluations, as well as direct and indirect approaches to community needs assessment). The evaluator's role must be similarly flexible.

What Have We Learned?

Although each reader will come away from this volume with a different sense of what has been learned over the past decade, we think several major substantive lessons are worth mentioning:

1. *Effects of programs or policies are likely to be small but nonetheless may be quite important.* Gueron provides convincing evidence that employment and training programs increase earnings and employment for many groups of welfare recipients by a relatively small amount, but the effects are usually large enough to offset program costs. Likewise, Lipsey reports that juvenile justice interventions (and human service interventions, in general) produce small but noteworthy effects. Although these impacts are frequently too small to detect in a single study, pooling studies (especially high-quality studies) provides intriguing evidence that a nontrivial fraction of juvenile delinquents can be rehabilitated. Similarly, Kennedy finds that direct cash housing assistance improves the housing conditions of some but by no means all low-income households who are offered this subsidy.

2. *Treatments—even those that carry the same label—vary considerably. Looking inside the "black box" of treatment will help us to understand why programs succeed or not.* This lesson is vividly illustrated by Sherman as he tries to unravel the puzzle represented by the fact that some types of sanctions reduce future criminal behavior, some have no effect, and some seem, paradoxically, to increase criminal behavior. Looking more closely at the features of individual treatment conditions, Sherman identifies severity, certainty, and celerity (speed) of the sanction as plausible explanations for the observed differences. Lipsey, in looking closely at juvenile delinquency treatments, distinguishes among their intensity, frequency, and duration.

One does not have to peer too deeply inside the black box of treatments to recognize that program variations can be substantial. Gueron's discussion of differences in state approaches to work-welfare programs reveals that numerous operational plans have been tested: some state initiatives entailed voluntary participation, and others were mandatory; some relied on work experience placements, and others used formal training programs. Although the jury is still out with respect to the relative effectiveness of these approaches, we can expect differences to exist, given the variability in their nature and content.

Another example of the importance of treatment specification is seen in Kennedy's discussion of different forms of direct cash assistance to low-income households. Central to his analysis of the effect of such assistance is the finding that different restrictions on the use of these subsidies (for example, minimum housing quality constraints or minimum rent constraints) produced marked differences in the types of housing improvements they stimulate.

3. *The effects of treatments are likely to vary substantially across different target groups and locales.* Too often prior evaluation efforts have focused on simplistic questions such as "Is the treatment effective?" This approach implies that successful programs will affect individuals uniformly. Several chapters included in this volume argue for a more explicit examination of interactions among specific types of treatments and target groups. Lipsey focuses on difficulties in identifying juvenile delinquents to treat. He argues that juvenile delinquency is a pattern of behavior that involves multiple repeat offenses. Because many teenagers act "in a delinquent manner on occasion" but do not repeat this behavior, it is difficult to determine who is truly a delinquent. Treating those who exhibit transient aberrant behavior will produce little in the way of program impact. Yet treating individuals who otherwise would continue a pattern of delinquency has a potential for producing effects. Kennedy deals with an analogous issue in the context of housing assistance.

Gueron and Sherman also illustrate the importance of clearly identifying target populations and distinguishing among subgroups within these populations. Gueron indicates that welfare recipients with the least prior employment experience tend to have the largest program-induced employment and earnings gains. Similarly, Sherman speculates about the likely differences in the response to sanctions for individuals with different patterns of offender careers, offender characteristics, opportunities to commit crimes, levels of commitment to criminal or conventional social values, and other related factors.

4. *Evaluations are often limited by small sample sizes, the implementation of weak and variable treatments, inadequate outcome variables, and poor research designs. These problems can be circumvented in many cases.* Without careful planning and rigorous designs, impact evaluations

can stack the deck against finding program effects. Lipsey is most explicit about this point and offers constructive solutions. Furthermore, Gueron's discussion shows that Lipsey's suggestions are feasible even in programs that are implemented under a variety of circumstances. Similarly, Yinger's discussion shows that improvements in measurement reduce the uncertainty of inference even in areas as complex as determining the level of discrimination in housing. From a mental health perspective, however, Ciarlo and Windle remind us that evaluation needs to be flexible if it is to answer the array of questions that could be asked by relevant constituency groups.

5. *Results of individual, well-executed evaluations contribute to our cumulative understanding of program theory, process, and outcomes.* Often applied research does not seem to be cumulative because it deals with practical answers to politically generated questions. The research reviewed in this volume shows that individual studies, when brought together and carefully synthesized, reveal patterns of evidence that can confidently confirm or refute major hypotheses. Furthermore, it is clear that a core of knowledge is accumulating about how and under what conditions programs work. Finally, as in other social sciences, evaluation studies serve at least two roles, they answer some questions and serve as the springboard for new inquiry. It seems that the past decade of evaluation effort, as judged by the contents of this volume, has taught us a great deal. And the prospects for the future are bright indeed.

Howard S. Bloom
David S. Cordray
Richard J. Light
Editors

Reference

Cordray, D. S., Bloom, H. S., and Light, R. J. (eds.). *Evaluation Practice in Review.* New Directions for Program Evaluation, no. 34. San Francisco: Jossey-Bass, 1987.

Howard S. Bloom is an associate professor in the Graduate School of Public Administration at New York University and is co-principal investigator of the National Job Training Partnership Act Study.

David S. Cordray is group director for federal evaluation policy within the Program-Evaluation and Methodology Division of the U.S. General Accounting Office, Washington, D.C.

Richard J. Light is a professor in the Graduate School of Education and the Kennedy School of Government at Harvard University.

A variety of work-welfare program arrangements yield effective treatments. Although their effects are small, they usually are large enough to justify program costs. Nevertheless, program effects vary considerably by type of program, by state, and by target group. To learn more about the nature and sources of these variations is perhaps the next great challenge in the development and testing of work-welfare programs.

Work-Welfare Programs

Judith M. Gueron

What have we learned about reforming welfare through work? Fortunately, we have learned a great deal, and this chapter will try to summarize the highlights of those findings. Clearly, this is a complex topic with a long history. To set the context for the findings, the chapter begins with a discussion of the Aid to Families with Dependent Children (AFDC) program and the evolution of the welfare reform debate. It then turns to what has been learned from recent state efforts to transform AFDC from an "entitlement" to benefits into a "bargain," where an AFDC grant carries some reciprocal obligation. In addition, the chapter discusses some of the implications of the recent findings for evaluation research and the relationship between evaluation and policy.

This chapter draws from an earlier paper by the author, "Reforming Welfare with Work," prepared for the Ford Foundation as part of its Project on Social Welfare Policy and the American Future. The research summarized here was supported by the Ford, Winthrop Rockefeller, and Claude Worthington Benedum foundations, the Congressional Research Service of the Library of Congress, and the states of Arizona, Arkansas, California, Florida, Illinois, Maine, Maryland, New Jersey, Texas, Virginia, and West Virginia. The research and the conclusions reached by the author, however, do not necessarily reflect the official position of the funders.

The AFDC Program and the Pressure for Reform

Public assistance programs in this country have always made a sharp distinction between people considered able to work and those judged appropriate for public support. Working-age men clearly fall into the former category—and only limited support has usually been available for this group through the welfare system. The aged and severely disabled fall into the latter. More controversy has surrounded poor single mothers, with a recent major shift in the emphasis given to ensuring the well-being of children and the importance of their parents' work and self-support.

When the AFDC program was adopted as part of the Social Security Act of 1935, it was regarded primarily as a means to provide assistance to poor children. The initial assumption was that only a small group of poor mothers would receive benefits on behalf of their children: widows and the wives of disabled workers who—like other women—were expected to stay at home and care for their children. The issue of work incentives did not arise since welfare eligibility was considered the result of hardship, not choice. The focus was on child welfare, and encouraging mothers to enter the workforce was not seen as a route toward that goal.

In recent years, several factors have affected public support for the AFDC program. First, in the 1960s and early 1970s, AFDC caseloads and costs grew rapidly, as did the proportion of the caseload headed by women who were divorced or never married. Second, the employment rates of all women—including single parents and women with very young children—increased dramatically, leading many to reconsider the equity and appropriateness of supporting welfare mothers who could be working. Third, while recent research confirms that most people use welfare for only short-term support, it also points to a not insignificant group for whom AFDC serves as a source of long-term assistance. The growing concern about the presumed negative effects of such dependency on adults and children has prompted intensified efforts to reach this group.

All these developments have affected public perceptions about the employability of welfare mothers and raised questions about whether the design of AFDC was not part of the problem.

Strategies for Reforming AFDC

All AFDC reform efforts have grappled with the challenge of providing adequate income while maintaining incentives for work and self-sufficiency, and doing both at reasonable cost. The lengthy debate has clarified the impossibility of simultaneously maximizing all these objectives, and identified some of the tradeoffs from different approaches.

During the period from the mid 1960s to the early 1970s, many efforts at increasing the employment of welfare recipients sought to do so through the provision of financial incentives to work within the AFDC program itself. As a first step, the 1967 amendments to the Social Security Act included provisions to reduce the rate at which welfare grants decreased (the implicit marginal "tax" rate) when recipients went to work. Then the debate shifted to the advantages of replacing AFDC with a universal, noncategorical, negative income tax (such as proposed in the Family Assistance Plan), which would guarantee a minimum income to all Americans—not only single-parent families, but all the working poor. It was hoped that this expanded coverage would not seriously reduce work effort but would lessen the incentives for family dissolution. However, some argued that the findings from several of the federally sponsored income maintenance experiments suggested that more generous work incentives, by increasing the size of the beneficiary population, would reduce, rather than increase, overall work effort. That is, the findings showed that the effect of changing the AFDC income floor and tax rate for people currently eligible was relatively small, but the impact on the number eligible was large. As a result, work reductions that were modest for the current caseload could become larger when combined with the work reductions of people newly eligible. Moreover, a substantial share of the additional cost of extending AFDC to two-parent households would simply go to replacing reduced earnings rather than raising income. To many people, this new evidence effectively killed the possibility for welfare reform through a comprehensive negative income tax approach.

As a result, the welfare reform proposals of both the Carter and Reagan administrations have included some form of a comprehensive work obligation, under which "employable" welfare recipients would have to accept a job or participate in some work-related activity. These approaches used mandatory requirements to provide an incentive—through the threat of a loss of welfare benefits—for work.

An early harbinger of this policy shift was the enactment of the Work Incentive (WIN) Program. Introduced as a discretionary program in 1967, WIN became mandatory in 1971; that is, as a condition of receiving AFDC benefits, all adult recipients with no preschool children or no specific problems that kept them at home were required to register with the state employment service, to participate in job training or job search activities, and to accept employment offers. Although in theory WIN imposed a participation obligation, it was in fact never funded at a level adequate to create a "slot" for each able-bodied person—the precondition for a real work test.

Under pressure to increase the work effort and reduce the AFDC rolls, both the Carter and Reagan proposals called for a redefinition of the welfare entitlement. The two designs showed striking—and usually overlooked—similarities. Both suggested that rights to welfare benefits be linked with obligations to work. However, an important difference appeared in the level and form of that aid. Under the Carter proposal, welfare recipients were guaranteed full-time Public Service Employment (PSE) jobs and paid wages. Under the Reagan administration's universal "workfare" plan, recipients would work in exchange for their grants with no compensation beyond the public assistance check (except for the limited reimbursement of expenses). In all states but those with the highest grants, the workfare formulation would lead to part-time work and continued low income.

The special appeal of this restatement of the AFDC "bargain" lies in its seeming reconciliation of the conflicting welfare policy objectives, at the same time as its potential for supporting a direct attack on the causes of poverty and dependency. The claimed advantages of this approach included:
- Strengthening work incentives and bringing AFDC into line with prevailing values
- Improving the employability of welfare recipients
- Providing useful public services
- Reducing the welfare rolls
- Providing psychological benefits to recipients and increasing public support for the AFDC program.

Critics challenged the ability of either the Carter or the Reagan proposal to deliver on these claims, noting:
- Given the existing delivery system and the nature of the welfare population, a large-scale participation and work requirement could not be enforced in a manner that met acceptable standards.
- It would not be possible to create a sufficient number of useful jobs that provided employment skills and did not displace regular workers.
- The program would increase rather than reduce costs. Workfare or PSE positions would not increase unsubsidized employment, because the economy did not generate enough jobs, and program services were of limited value. Moreover, welfare rolls would not be reduced, since a work obligation would neither deter applicants nor instill a missing work ethic.
- Public employee and other groups would not accept the supplementation of the work force by unpaid or low-paid public assistance recipients.

Although many of these criticisms were directed both at the Carter and Reagan proposals, welfare advocates were more sympathetic to the Carter PSE approach than to the Reagan workfare model. In addition, to the extent that the list of required activities was expanded to include education and training and the amount of support services increased, advocates were more supportive, since the balance of obligation and opportunity appeared to shift.

Ultimately, the high cost of the Carter administration's proposal—the Congressional Budget Office put a price tag of over $15 billion a year on the Program for Better Jobs and Income—led to its rejection. The Reagan administration's 1981 version was treated more favorably, but here too Congress did not mandate a national program. The states, in implementing workfare, have made further changes, transforming it from a straight work requirement, by which recipients "pay back" society, to an obligation directed as much at assisting in the transition off the rolls as in fulfilling an obligation while on welfare.

Lessons from the 1980s: The Demonstration of State Work-Welfare Initiatives

Congress, in passing the Omnibus Budget Reconciliation Act of 1981 (OBRA), reflected both a growing consensus on the need to increase work and self-support, and uncertainty about the feasibility and effectiveness of the universal workfare proposal. As a result, the legislation gave states a chance to experiment, albeit within a context of sharply reduced funding.

In 1982, the Manpower Demonstration Research Corporation (MDRC) began a five-year social experiment examining new state work initiatives. Because of the changed environment since 1981, and the lack of much reliable earlier research, the remainder of this chapter focuses on this post-1981 research.

MDRC's Demonstration of State Work-Welfare initiatives is a series of large-scale evaluations in eight states and smaller-scale studies in three additional states. The project is funded by private foundations and the participating states, which, in general, received no special operating funds. As a result, the project is not a test of centrally developed and funded reform proposals but of programs designed at the state level in the new environment of OBRA flexibility and constrained funding.

To ensure that the project produces findings of national relevance, the eight states are broadly representative of national variations in local conditions, administrative arrangements, and AFDC benefit levels. In the participating states, for example, AFDC benefit levels for a family of three in 1982 ranged from a low of $140 per month in Arkansas to a high of $526 in California. Demonstration locations include all or part of several large urban areas—San Diego, Baltimore, and Chicago—and a number of large multicounty areas spanning both urban and rural centers—Arkansas, Maine, New Jersey, Virginia, and West Virginia.

The demonstration tests not one program model, but a range of strategies, reflecting differences in philosophy, objectives, and funding. Some programs are limited to one or two activities, while others offer a wider mix. A few are voluntary, but most require participation as a condition of receiving benefits.

In designing their programs, many states turned to job search activities and to unpaid work experience. The job search strategy is based on the assumption that many welfare recipients are currently employable, but fail to find jobs because they do not know how (or are not sufficiently motivated) to look for them.

In programs that mandate unpaid work experience, two versions are commonly used. Under the Community Work Experience Program (CWEP), or workfare, version, work hours are determined by dividing the AFDC grant by the minimum wage. The work requirements can be either limited in duration or open-ended—that is, they last as long as the recipients remain on the welfare rolls. Under the WIN work experience version, the number of hours worked is unrelated to the grant level and participation is generally limited to thirteen weeks.

Contrary to some expectations, the states in the MDRC demonstration did not choose to implement universal workfare. Instead, required job search was the more widely used approach. Only West Virginia operated a full workfare program with no limit on a recipient's length of participation. Furthermore, this program was directed primarily to men receiving assistance under the AFDC program for unemployed heads of two-parent families (AFDC-U) rather than to women on AFDC.

Other states (Arkansas, California, Illinois) established a two-stage program of job search followed by a limited (usually three-month) work obligation for those who did not find unsubsidized jobs. Virginia required job search of everyone and offered short-term CWEP as one option among other mandatory services. Maryland offered a range of education and training options (including job search assistance and unpaid work experience), with choices tailored to individual needs and preferences. Two states—New Jersey and Maine—established voluntary on-the-job training programs with private employers, using grant diversion as the funding mechanism.

The projects varied in scale. Although most were large, none covered the full AFDC caseload. Five operated in only part of the state. Most were directed to women with school-age children—the only group traditionally required to register with WIN—who typically represent about one-third of the adults heading AFDC cases. Within that category, programs often targeted different groups—for example, welfare applicants or recipients, or people receiving welfare through AFDC or through the AFDC-U program.

The states also had different objectives. Some placed relatively more emphasis on human capital development and helping welfare recipients obtain better jobs and achieve long-term self-sufficiency. Others stressed direct job placement and welfare savings. The states also varied in the extent to which they have emphasized and enforced a participation requirement. While most planned to increase participation above the levels achieved in WIN, few clearly articulated a goal of full or universal participation.

Interim Findings from the State Work-Welfare Initiatives. The evaluation is structured as a series of three-year studies in each state and, because of the phase-in schedules of state activities, extends over a five-year period. Final results are now available from five of the programs—in Arkansas; San Diego, California; Virginia; West Virginia; and Baltimore, Maryland. Partial results are available from most of the others. For a more detailed discussion of the interim findings, see Gueron (1986, 1987). The final reports now available are Friedlander, Hoerz, Quint, and others (1985); Friedlander, Hoerz, Long, and others (1985); Friedlander and others (1986); Goldman and others (1986); and Riccio and others (1986). Interim findings from the studies are included in the following reports: Auspos, Ball, Goldman, and Gueron (1985); Ball and others (1984); Goldman and others (1984); Manpower Demonstration Research Corporation (1985); Price and others (1985); Quint, Goldman, and Gueron (1984); Quint and others (1984, 1986). The MRDC demonstration addresses four basic questions.

Question 1: Is it feasible to impose obligations—or participation requirements—as a condition of welfare receipt? Before 1981, welfare employment programs—both the WIN Program and several special demonstrations—were generally unable to establish meaningful work-related obligations for recipients. A major question at the outset of the MDRC demonstration was whether the existing bureaucracies would have better success.

In some cases, the answer was yes. Typically, within six to nine months of registering with the new program, about half of the AFDC group had participated in some activity, and substantial additional numbers had left the welfare rolls and the program. Thus, for example, within nine months of welfare application in San Diego, all but a small proportion—9 percent of the AFDC and 6 percent of the AFDC-U applicants—had either left welfare, become employed, were no longer in the program, or had fulfilled all of the program requirements. Comparable rates were about 25 percent in other states, indicating a somewhat less strict enforcement of the participation requirement. This represents a major management achievement and reflects a change in institutions and staff attitudes.

However, given the financial constraints under which states have been operating, one should not exaggerate the level of services provided or the intensity and scope of the work obligation imposed. The major activity was job search, a relatively short-term and modest intervention. And when workfare was required, it was almost always a time-limited obligation—usually thirteen weeks. Thus, programs were relatively inexpensive, with average costs per eligible person ranging from $165 in Arkansas to $1,050 in Maryland.

Question 2: What do workfare-type programs look like in practice, and how do welfare recipients themselves judge the fairness of mandatory requirements? Much of the workfare debate hinges on the nature of the worksite experience; that is, whether the positions are punitive and make-work or whether the work produces useful goods and services, provides dignity, and develops work skills. MDRC addressed these questions using an in-depth interview with random samples of supervisors and participants in six states. Results suggested that:

1. The jobs were generally entry-level positions in maintenance or clerical fields, park service, and human services.

2. While the positions did not primarily develop skills, they were not make-work, either. Supervisors judged the work important and indicated that participants' productivity and attendance were similar to those of most entry-level workers.

3. A large proportion of the participants were satisfied with their positions and with coming to work, and believed that they were making a useful contribution.

4. Many participants, however, believed that their employers got the better end of the bargain, or that they were underpaid for their work. In brief, they would have preferred a paid job.

These findings suggest that most states did not design or implement CWEP or workfare with a punitive intent. This approach may explain results from the worksite survey that indicated that the majority of participants in most states shared the view that a work requirement was fair.

In addition, the findings are consistent with other studies that show that the poor want to work. As one of MDRC's field researchers observed, these workfare programs did not create the work ethic, they found it.

Although this evidence is striking, it should not be used to draw conclusions about the quality of programs—or the reactions of welfare recipients—if workfare-type requirements are implemented on a larger scale, are differently designed, or are of longer duration.

Questions 3 and 4: Do these initiatives make a difference? Do they reduce the welfare rolls and costs or increase employment and earnings? How do program benefits compare to costs? Experience suggests that these questions are very difficult to answer. The work of Bane and Ellwood (1983) and Ellwood (1986) shows that, contrary to popular conceptions, half of all welfare applicants normally move off the rolls within two years. Thus, if a study estimates impacts or cost savings based only on the performance of program participants—for example, their job placements—it will overstate program accomplishments by taking credit for those who would have found jobs on their own. The challenge in assessing program impacts is to distinguish program-induced changes from the normal dynamics of welfare turnover and the regular labor market behavior of this population. As discussed in a later section, making such a distinction requires data on what people would have done in the absence of the program; that is, data on a control group.

In eight of the states studied, the research is structured to provide such a control group. In an unusual display of commitment to high standards of program evaluation, Human Resources Commissioners from these states actively cooperated with the random assignment of over 35,000 individuals to different groups, some participating in the program and some placed in a control group receiving limited or no services (see Gueron, 1985).

To assess the impact and benefit-cost results of these experiments is like looking at a glass and characterizing it as half full or half empty. Depending on one's perspective, one can either point to accomplishments or find a basis for caution. In any event, the findings are complex and require a careful reading.

First, the results dispel the notion that employment and training interventions do not work. Four of the five programs for which studies have been completed produced positive employment results for AFDC women. The one program that did not was the workfare initiative in West Virginia, where high unemployment severely limited job opportunities.

In San Diego, for example, mandatory job search followed by short-term CWEP increased the employment rate over the 15 months of follow-up by six percentage points (from 55 to 61 percent). Average total earnings during the same period went up by $700 per experimental, representing a 23 percent increase over the control group's average earnings. (See Table 1.) One unusual feature of the San Diego study was the simultaneous random assignment to two experimental treatments: job search alone and job search followed by CWEP. The results showed job search alone also had positive impacts, but the findings were less consistent and the gains in earnings smaller than for the combined program.

Roughly half of the earnings gains in San Diego came about because more women worked, and half because they obtained longer-lasting jobs or jobs with better pay or longer hours. The employment gains persisted, although at a somewhat reduced level, throughout the almost one and a half years of follow-up. (In contrast, the program produced minimal or no sustained employment effects for the primarily male group receiving AFDC-U assistance.)

Table 1. Summary of the Impact of AFDC Work/Welfare Programs in San Diego, Baltimore, Arkansas, Virginia, and West Virginia

Outcome[a]	Experimentals	Controls	Difference	Decrease or Increase
San Diego—Applicants				
Ever employed during 15 months	61.0%	55.4%	+5.6%***	+10%
Average total earnings during 15 months	$3,802	$3,102	+$700***	+23%
Ever received AFDC payments during 18 months	83.9%	84.3%	−0.4%	0%
Average total AFDC payments received during 18 months	$3,409	$3,697	−$288**	−8%
Baltimore—Applicants and Recipients				
Ever employed during 12 months	51.2%	44.2%	+7.0%***	+16%
Average total earnings during 12 months	$1,935	$1,759	+$176	+10%
Ever received AFDC payments during 15 months	94.9%	95.1%	−0.2%	0%
Average total AFDC payments received during 15 months	$3,058	$3,064	−$6	0%
Arkansas—Applicants and Recipients				
Ever employed during 6 months	18.8%	14.0%	+4.8%**	+34%
Average total earnings during 6 months	$291	$213	+$78*	+37%
Ever received AFDC payments during 9 months	72.8%	75.9%	−3.1%	−4%
Average total AFDC payments received during 9 months	$772	$865	−$93***	−11%

Table 1. *(continued)*

Outcome[a]	Experimentals	Controls	Difference	Decrease or Increase
Virginia—Applicants and Recipients				
Ever employed during 9 months	43.8%	40.5%	+3.3%*	+8%
Average total earnings during 9 months	$1,119	$1,038	+$81	+8%
Ever received AFDC payments during 12 months	86.0%	86.1%	-0.1%	0%
Average total AFDC payments received during 12 months	$1,923	$2,007	-$84**	-4%
West Virginia—Applicants and Recipients				
Ever employed during 15 months	22.3%	22.7%	-0.4%	-2%
Average total earnings during 15 months	$713	$712	$0	0%
Ever received AFDC payments during 21 months	96.8%	96.0%	+0.8%	+1%
Average total AFDC payments received during 21 months	$2,681	$2,721	-$40	-1%

Notes: These data include zero values for sample members not employed and for sample members not receiving welfare payments. The estimates are regression-adjusted using ordinary least squares, controlling for prerandom assignment characteristics of sample members. There may be some discrepancies in calculating experimental-control differences due to rounding.

[a] The length of follow-up varied by outcomes and state. Employment and earnings were measured by calendar quarters. To assure that preprogram earnings were excluded from the impact estimates, the follow-up period began after the quarter of random assignment. In contrast, AFDC benefits were tracked for quarters beginning with the actual month of random assignment. As a result, the follow-up period for AFDC benefits was at least three months longer than that for employment and earnings.

*Denotes statistical significance at the 10 percent level; ** at the 5 percent level; and *** at the 1 percent level.

Source: Final reports from programs in San Diego, Arkansas, Baltimore, Virginia, and West Virginia.

Roughly half of the earnings gains in San Diego came about because more women worked, and half because they obtained longer-lasting jobs or jobs with better pay or longer hours. The employment gains persisted, although at a somewhat reduced level, throughout the almost one and a half years of follow-up. (In contrast, the program produced minimal or no sustained employment effects for the primarily male group receiving AFDC-U assistance.)

Roughly similar employment gains were obtained in Arkansas, Maryland, and Virginia, although target group and control group earnings varied dramatically across the states.

As indicated in Table 1, the findings were quite different in West Virginia, where the relatively pure workfare program led to no increase in employment and earnings. Although many explanations are possible—including the design of the program or the characteristics of the women served—the most likely is that foreseen by the program's planners, who did not anticipate any employment gains in a highly rural state with the nation's highest unemployment rate. This case is a useful reminder that there are two sides to the labor market. Welfare employment programs focus on the supply side. In extreme cases, when the demand is not there, the provision of work experience and a change in the terms of the welfare "bargain" may simply not be enough to affect employment levels.

The programs also led to some welfare savings, although compared to their effects on employment and earnings, these were less consistent. In San Diego, for example, over 18 months, average welfare payments to AFDC experimentals were $288 below those paid to controls, a reduction in welfare outlays of almost 8 percent. As shown in Table 1, similar reductions occurred in Arkansas and Virginia, although not in Maryland and West Virginia. However, there was no evidence that once people had applied for welfare, they were deterred from that process by the work obligation.

A third encouraging piece of information is that the programs were most helpful for some of the most disadvantaged members of the welfare caseload. For example, where examined so far in the study, employment increases were usually much greater for women on AFDC than men on AFDC-U and for those with no prior employment compared to those with a recent work history. Although women and the recently unemployed were still less likely to be working and more likely to be on welfare than their more advantaged counterparts, employment requirements and services helped narrow the gap.

Finally, when effects were compared to costs, results were generally positive. An examination of the programs' effects on the government budget shows that, not surprisingly, such initiatives cost money up front, but in general the investment pays off in future budget savings within five years. For example, in San Diego, an average dollar spent on the program for AFDC women led to estimated budget savings—over a five-year period—of over two dollars. Programs in Arkansas and Virginia also led to budget savings, while in Maryland and West Virginia there were some net costs.

The research also offers some unusual findings on the distribution of benefits across federal, state, and county budgets, a question not often addressed in benefit-cost studies. In San Diego, where a detailed study was conducted, all three levels of government ultimately gained under the particular funding formulas and matching arrangements in place. However, the federal government bore more than half of the costs and enjoyed the greatest net savings. Indeed, had there been no federal funds —or had there been substantially less—the state and county would have had no financial incentive to run these programs. These findings highlight the importance of continued federal support to encourage states to undertake welfare employment initiatives that ultimately may prove cost-effective to operate.

Another way to look at program benefits and costs is to examine them from the perspectives of the groups targeted for program participation—that is, those who might have earned more as a result of the program, but who also might have lost money because of reductions in welfare and other transfer payments. In most cases, the AFDC women came out ahead, the exceptions being in (1) Arkansas, where almost any employment—in such a low-grant state—led to case closings, and (2) West Virginia, where there were no earnings gains. For men on AFDC-U, the story was very different—with overall losses, not gains— from the programs as reductions in welfare and other transfer payments exceeded increases in earnings.

What about the empty half of the glass? In what way do the results suggest caution? It is important to note that, while the programs produced changes, the magnitudes of those changes were relatively modest. Quarterly employment increases were between 3 and 9 percentage points. Earnings increased $110 to $560 a year on average (including zero earners). Thus, while it is worthwhile to operate these programs, they offer no quick cure for poverty.

Issues and Lessons. Results to date from the MDRC work-welfare demonstration suggest the following major lessons.

It is feasible, under certain conditions and at the scale the demonstration programs were implemented, to tie welfare receipt to participation obligations. However, just as striking as this increase in participation is the nature of the obligation. In most cases, it has been confined to job search, with workfare used only in a limited way for a relatively small number of people.

A number of quite different approaches to structuring and targeting work-welfare programs will yield effective treatments. Overall, MDRC's results do not point to a uniform approach that merits national replication. Instead, one of the most striking characteristics of the work-welfare programs is their diversity—in population, conditions, and outcomes. A key explanation for the successful implementation of these initiatives may indeed be that states were given an opportunity to experiment and felt more ownership in the programs than they did in the earlier WIN Program, which was characterized by highly prescriptive central direction.

In cases in which states chose to operate mandatory workfare, the interim results do not support the strongest claims of critics or advocates. Despite critics' fears, workfare as implemented in the 1980s is more likely to be designed to provide useful work experience than simply to enforce a *quid pro quo*—although both objectives may be present.

A consistent lesson from the results available so far—and from earlier evaluations as well—is that program impacts are greater for the enrollees without recent work experience. This lesson does not mean that these hard-to-employ groups had the highest placement rates and levels of postprogram employment. On the contrary, the levels were higher for individuals who were more "job-ready."

Although seemingly contradictory, this pattern is consistent with the dynamics of the welfare population. For many, welfare receipt is only a temporary source of aid. A program achieving high placement rates by working with people who would have found jobs on their own may look more successful but, in fact, may not have accomplished much. In contrast, a program working with those who would do poorly on their own may have less impressive placement or employment rates, but may have brought about a major change in behavior. This result was the case in four of the states; the exception was West Virginia.

Overall the programs led to relatively modest increases in employment, which in some cases translated into even smaller welfare savings. Nonetheless, the changes were usually large enough to justify the program's cost, although this finding varied by state and target group. For those accustomed to grandiose claims for social programs, the outcomes for the current work-welfare programs—as well as for other welfare employment efforts—may look small. With gains that are not dramatic and limited savings, the programs do not promise to be a cure for poverty or a shortcut to balancing the budget. As a result, some critics have rejected these approaches, claiming that a 3 to 9 percentage point gain in employment or an 8 to 36 percent increase in earnings are unsatisfactory. There are, however, several reasons to conclude otherwise.

First, people are always strongly tempted to search for a simple solution to a complex problem. The welfare debate is filled with this kind of rhetoric and, now faced with the reality of limited gains, the tendency for those who once advocated requirements and deterrence is to lurch toward another "solution" for which there is no similar evidence. Yet, in an environment where reliable findings on the effect of social policy are rare, the striking feature of these results for mandatory work programs is that most of the effects—across a wide range of environments—are positive.

Second, in view of the fact that the demonstration measured changes for samples that were representative of large groups in the welfare caseload, results in the range of 5 percentage points take on added significance. It should be kept in mind that outcomes are expressed as averages for a wide range of individuals, some of whom gained little or nothing from the program (including those who never received any services) and others who may have gained more. Thus, even relatively small changes, multiplied by large numbers of people, have considerable policy significance.

Third, the targeting lessons from the demonstration suggest ways to make these programs more effective and provide evidence that some groups benefit by more substantial amounts than others.

Fourth, it is possible that short-term effects underestimate longer-term gains, if attitudes toward AFDC shifted as the concept of reciprocal obligations became more widespread. (On the other side, evidence also exists that, in some cases, initially positive effects may decay over time.)

Fifth, the demonstration's benefit-cost findings suggest that, within a relatively short time, program savings often offset costs, a balance that represents about as much as a social program can be expected to achieve. Although previous smaller-scale tests of special programs have produced cost-effective results, the demonstration provides the first solid evidence of such outcomes in a major ongoing service delivery system, the WIN Demonstration Program.

Unanswered Questions. These state initiatives provide a wealth of information about the implementation and effectiveness of alternative approaches to reforming welfare with work, but they leave unanswered a number of questions about the design and scale of programs.

The results summarized in this paper are for programs that have participation obligations of limited intensity, cost, or duration. They primarily required job search and short-term work experience. One unanswered question is whether more costly, comprehensive programs—providing either more services or longer obligations—would have greater effects.

Several states—for example, California in the Greater Avenues for Independence (GAIN) legislation, and Massachusetts in the Employment and Training (ET) Choices program—are using or plan to provide more intensive services or requirements, including educational remediation and training, and to complement these with extensive child care services. Another more intensive approach is Supported Work, a program offering paid transitional work experience under conditions of close supervision, peer support, and, generally, increasing responsibilities. Supported Work was tested as a voluntary program and found effective for women with histories of long-term welfare dependency (Manpower Demonstration Research Corporation, 1980). Although the incremental return to larger investments is not clear, the persistence of dependency for many, even after job search, or short-term workfare, provides a rationale for states to offer more intensive services, while evaluating them to see whether they lead to long-term rewards.

A second open question concerns the broader implications of an ongoing participation requirement for family formation, the well-being of children, and attitudes toward work. It is important to note that child care was not a major issue in these programs, since their requirements were mostly short-term and limited mainly to women with school-age children. However, the availability and quality of child care would be much more important if either of these conditions changed, or if the programs made even larger differences in the rate at which women moved out of the home and into permanent jobs.

A third unanswered question is whether relatively low-cost mandatory programs will prove effective for the most disadvantaged groups of welfare recipients, those facing major barriers to employment (such as persons with substantial language problems or educational deficiencies). Although evidence exists that the programs have a larger impact on recipients who have some obstacles to employment—as opposed to the more job-ready, who will find employment on their own—more study is required to determine whether there is a threshold below which more intensive assistance is needed (see Friedlander and Long, 1987).

A fourth unanswered question concerns the feasibility of operating larger-scale universal programs, and whether they would have the same results. Although the pre-1980 work mandates often foundered against legal, political, and bureaucratic obstacles, the more recent large-scale initiatives described in this chapter were implemented more smoothly (see Gueron and Nathan, 1985). However, it is not clear whether work programs can be extended to an even greater share of the AFDC caseload (including the majority of AFDC women with younger children) without compromising quality, encountering political or administrative resistance, or raising broader issues, such as whether welfare recipients would displace regular workers either during or after the program. Also, as the West Virginia findings suggest, in rural areas with very weak economic conditions, workfare serves as a subsidized job program, not as a transition to unsubsidized employment. A major unanswered question is the more precise relationship between program effectiveness and economic conditions, and whether this relationship is affected by the scale of the program.

In addition, all the results described in this chapter refer to a relatively short-term follow-up. Whether these results persist, increase, or decay is important in judging the potential of the work-welfare approach.

Finally, although substantial information exists on the effectiveness of these programs, it remains unclear whether the achievements come from the services provided or from the mandatory aspect of the programs. Other studies show that voluntary job search and work experience programs also are effective for AFDC women. See Manpower Demonstration Research Corporation (1980) and Wolfhagen (1983). Although the distinction between mandatory and voluntary programs is sometimes not as great as one might think—since most nominally mandatory programs seek voluntary compliance and involvement—some differences exist and their importance remains uncertain.

Impact of the Work-Welfare Research on Policy

The findings on welfare employment initiatives just reported have had a substantial impact on public policy at the federal, state, and local levels, both because of the reliability of the findings and the degree of current interest in these issues. For example, the benefit-cost analyses have added some realism to the Congressional debate and budget estimates of the potential savings from this approach. The findings on the distribution of net costs by level of government have influenced legislative proposals on funding formulas and cost sharing. The levels of participation have clarified the potential for extending programs to cover a greater proportion of the welfare caseload. The overall impact findings have helped convince legislators that welfare employment programs may actually be saving—rather than wasting—public resources.

In addition, the findings have helped demystify workfare and move the debate from rhetoric closer to reality. Findings on the opinions of welfare recipients proved important, as did those on the value of the goods and services produced in the workfare jobs. Finally, the impact findings have led to new programs at the state level. The interim findings for San Diego were prominent in the debate about California's statewide GAIN program. Findings on the differential impact on subgroups within the welfare population were used to specifically match subgroups to services.

Lessons for Evaluation Research

The preceding sections of this chapter discussed what we have learned about work-welfare initiatives and the impact of these lessons on public policy. But the research also has important implications for program evaluators, and for administrators seeking to assess program effectiveness.

First, the results suggest the importance of a broad research agenda. The politics of work-welfare are highly charged. This discussion is not just about alternative programmatic approaches, but also about values and the complex issue of social responsibility. The evaluation has had to address many questions: bureaucratic response, the impact on the welfare rolls, and program net costs and their distribution, as well as more complex issues of values and ethics.

Second, the research on state work-welfare initiatives was conducted on a large scale and within the regular delivery system. The successful implementation of the research points to the potential to embed rigorous designs within real-world operations. Although this goal was very challenging and limited what could be tested, as a result the findings are particularly valuable. The lessons are derived not from a laboratory project but instead are directly generalizable to the existing delivery system. Conducting a study this way poses special requirements, but it also gives researchers an unusual opportunity to engage administrators and staff in the learning process. Thus, although setting up the project may be more difficult, the gap between presenting findings and formulating policy may be more easily bridged.

Third, the results to date confirm the importance of using an evaluation design with a randomly selected control group. The relatively modest impacts encompass subtle differences in outcomes over time, and across subgroups and locations. If participants had been compared to individuals in different counties or to selected nonparticipants, rather than to a control group, these effects might have gone undetected or their validity been questioned (see Friedlander and others, 1986).

Findings from the demonstration also show clearly how administrative data—that is, "gross" impacts—can overstate true program effects. For example, data for San Diego show that 78 percent of the experimental group were on welfare when the study began, and only 35 percent remained on the rolls by the sixth quarter of follow-up. In the absence of a control group, one might (1) assume that the program led to a 43 percent reduction in the rolls, (2) multiply that by the average grant, and (3) claim very large welfare savings. In fact, by the end of the sixth quarter, data from the control group indicate that most of the departures from welfare would have occurred anyway; the net program impact was only about 1 percentage point.

Estimates based on job placement or employment rates can be equally misleading. For example, Table 1 shows that over 60 percent of the experimentals in San Diego were employed at some point over the follow-up period. If one assumes that all this employment was caused by the program—and one multiplies the number of placements or employed individuals by the average reduction in grant payments that takes place after employment—the result is extremely large welfare savings. Instead,

Table 1 reveals that over 55 percent of the controls worked at some time during the same period *without* participating in the program. The real gain is notable, but much smaller. Unfortunately, most administrators only have data on program participants and not on a control group. It will be tempting for them to look at administrative data and assume that all changes are program achievements, but the research data suggests how misleading this can be.

The study of recent work-welfare initiatives was not only unusual in the scope and rigor of the analysis, but also in the funding arrangement. The research is supported by a challenge grant from the Ford Foundation, with about 50 percent of the funds for each state study coming from local foundations or the states (which sometimes used special federal demonstration grants). Although difficult to establish, this kind of partnership between states and foundations may help account for the strong support from state officials in meeting research requirements and for their high level of interest in the research results.

Finally, an important lesson from the work-welfare research concerns the politics of presenting reliable evidence of relatively limited impacts in an environment of exaggerated claims. Studies of welfare-employment programs consistently indicate that effects are likely to be small when measured against expectations. Yet an important conclusion from the research is that small can be enough. The challenge facing evaluators is to reconcile what is learned about what can be achieved, with the inevitable hunt for a "solution." The pressure to simplify and overstate is strong, but reliable evaluation evidence is crucial in guiding the policy debate.

References

Auspos, P., with Ball, J., Goldman, B., and Gueron, J. *Maine: Interim Findings from a Grant Diversion Program.* New York: Manpower Demonstration Research Corporation, 1985.

Ball, J., with Hamilton, G., Hoerz, G., Goldman, B., and Gueron, J. *West Virginia: Interim Findings on the Community Work Experience Demonstrations.* New York: Manpower Demonstration Research Corporation, 1984.

Ball, J., and Wolfhagen, C., with Gerould, D., and Solnick, L. *The Participation of Private Businesses as Work Sponsors in the Youth Entitlement Demonstration.* New York: Manpower Demonstration Research Corporation, 1981.

Bane, M. J., and Ellwood, D. T. *The Dynamics of Dependence: The Routes to Self-Sufficiency.* Cambridge, Mass.: Urban Systems Research and Engineering, Inc., 1983.

Ellwood, D. T. *Targeting "Would-Be" Long-Term Recipients of AFDC.* Princeton, N.J.: Mathematica Policy Research, Inc., 1986.

Friedlander, D., Erickson, M., Hamilton, G., Knox, V., with Goldman, B., Gueron, J., and Long, D. *West Virginia: Final Report on the Community Work Experience Demonstrations.* New York: Manpower Demonstration Research Corporation, 1986.

Friedlander, D., Hoerz, G., Long, D., Quint, J., with Goldman, B., and Gueron, J. *Maryland: Final Report on the Employment Initiatives Evaluation.* New York: Manpower Demonstration Research Corporation, 1985.
Friedlander, D., Hoerz, G., Quint, J., Riccio, J., with Goldman, B., Gueron, J., and Long, D. *Arkansas: Final Report on the WORK Program in Two Counties.* New York: Manpower Demonstration Research Corporation, 1985.
Friedlander, D., and Long, D. *A Study of Performance Measures and Subgroup Impacts in Three Welfare Employment Programs.* New York: Manpower Demonstration Research Corporation, 1987.
Goldman, B., Friedlander, D., Gueron, J., Long, D., with Hamilton, G., and Hoerz, G. *Findings from the San Diego Job Search and Work Experience Demonstration.* New York: Manpower Demonstration Research Corporation, 1985.
Goldman, B., Friedlander, D., Long, D., with Erickson, M., and Gueron, J. *Final Report on the San Diego Job Search and Work Experience Demonstration.* New York: Manpower Demonstration Research Corporation, 1986.
Goldman, B., Gueron, J., Ball, J., Price, M., with Friedlander, D., and Hamilton, G. *Preliminary Findings from the San Diego Job Search and Work Experience Demonstration.* New York: Manpower Demonstration Research Corporation, 1984.
Gueron, J. M. "The Demonstration of State Work/Welfare Initiatives." In R. F. Boruch and W. Wothke (eds.), *Randomization and Field Experimentation.* New Directions for Program Evaluation, no. 28. San Francisco: Jossey-Bass, 1985.
Gueron, J. M. *Work Initiatives for Welfare Recipients: Lessons from a Multi-State Experiment.* New York: Manpower Demonstration Research Corporation, 1986.
Gueron, J. M. "Reforming Welfare with Work." Occasional Paper no. 2. New York: Ford Foundation Project on Social Welfare Policy and the American Future, 1987.
Gueron, J., and Nathan, R. "The MDRC Work/Welfare Project: Objectives, Status, Significance." *Policy Studies Review,* 1985, *4* (3), 417-432.
Manpower Demonstration Research Corporation. *Summary and Findings of the National Supported Work Demonstration.* Cambridge, Mass.: Ballinger, 1980.
Manpower Demonstration Research Corporation. *Baseline Paper on the Evaluation of the WIN Demonstration Program in Cook County, Illinois.* New York: Manpower Demonstration Research Corporation, 1985.
Price, M., with Ball, J., Goldman, B., Gruber, D., Gueron, J., and Hamilton, G. *Interim Findings from the Virginia Employment Services Program.* New York: Manpower Demonstration Research Corporation, 1985.
Quint, J., with Ball, J., Goldman, B., Gueron, J., and Hamilton, G. *Interim Findings from the Maryland Employment Initiatives Programs.* New York: Manpower Demonstration Research Corporation, 1984.
Quint, J., with Goldman, B., and Gueron, J. *Interim Findings from the Arkansas WIN Demonstration Program.* New York: Manpower Demonstration Research Corporation, 1984.
Quint, J., Guy, C., with Hoerz, G., Hamilton, G., Ball, J., Goldman, B., and Gueron, J. *Interim Findings from the Illinois WIN Demonstration Program in Cook County.* New York: Manpower Demonstration Research Corporation, 1986.
Riccio, J., Cave, G., Freedman, S., Price, M., with Friedlander, D., Goldman, B., Gueron, J., and Long, D. *Final Report on the Virginia Employment Services Program.* New York: Manpower Demonstration Research Corporation, 1986.
Wolfhagen, C., with Goldman, B. *Job Search Strategies: Lessons from the Louisville WIN Laboratory Project.* New York: Manpower Demonstration Research Corporation, 1983.

Judith M. Gueron is president of the Manpower Demonstration Research Corporation (MDRC), New York City. Dr. Gueron has directed numerous large-scale national studies and is the principal investigator of the Demonstration of Work/Welfare Initiatives, a multistate evaluation of welfare employment programs. Dr. Gueron received her doctorate in economics from Harvard University and has published extensively in the field of welfare and employment.

Evidence from evaluation of low-income housing assistance programs in this country indicates that: those which use existing housing are less expensive than those which require new housing construction, but existing housing programs do not reach people in the worst housing. Program effects are relatively small, except for people who are induced to change their housing, and the effect for others is primarily to reduce their rent burden.

Direct Cash Low-Income Housing Assistance

Stephen D. Kennedy

Direct cash, low-income housing assistance programs pay for all or part of the rents of low-income households renting in the private market. These are distinguished from simple income transfers by tying the assistance payment to requirements that recipient housing meet certain standards or to the amounts that recipients pay for rent, or both. They are distinguished from construction programs by subsidizing recipients in the private market instead of in units specifically constructed as low-income housing. Although there are a number of possible direct cash assistance programs, the major current version is the Section 8 Existing Housing Program. As now structured, this program pays for gross rent (including scheduled utilities) in excess of 30 percent of recipient income for recipients living in program-acceptable housing. The amount of the subsidy is limited by caps placed on recipient gross rents by the U.S. Department of Housing and Urban Development (HUD) and by the local Public Housing Authorities (PHAs) that administer the program.

Evaluation of direct cash assistance has focused on comparison with two major alternatives—expanded welfare payments or construction programs. Expanded welfare programs eliminate housing programs per se, and absorb assistance into general cash transfers. Construction pro-

grams subsidize recipients in units specifically constructed for low-income housing. The two major variants include
- Public housing, in which the local PHA builds (Conventional) or contracts to have built (Turnkey) housing projects, which are then operated by the PHA and offered to eligible tenants at reduced rents.
- Section 236, Section 23 (New Construction) and Section 8 (New Construction), in which HUD subsidizes private developers, who build and operate projects for low-income tenants at agreed-on (subsidized) rents.

This chapter discusses what is known and what is not known in terms of the relative costs and impacts of these alternative programs. The findings reported here are largely based on analyses of the five major data collection and analysis efforts undertaken by HUD during the 1970s, plus interim results from one ongoing evaluation. These six efforts are briefly described below.

1. *The Administrative Agency Experiment (AAE),* conducted by Abt Associates, collected extensive information about 15,000 direct cash assistance program applicants and recipients in eight cities between 1973 and 1976 (see Hamilton, 1979). The major concerns of the AAE were, first, the administrative feasibility of a direct cash assistance program and, second, examination of differences in costs and outcomes associated with variations in program operations and local market conditions. Because the AAE was primarily concerned with administrative feasibility, it did not impose any design on the variation in agency operations or include a control group. As a result, analysis is hampered by the self-selection of applicants and recipients and by problems inherent in disentangling the effects of variations in local market conditions from variations in program operations.

2. *The Housing Allowance Demand Experiment,* also conducted by Abt Associates, collected quite extensive information about 3,400 direct cash assistance program applicants and recipients in two sites, Pittsburgh and Phoenix, between 1973 and 1977 (see Kennedy, 1980). The focus of the Demand Experiment was recipient outcomes under alternative direct cash assistance programs. It was based on an experimental design involving random assignment of a probability sample of eligible households across seventeen program variations, plus control groups. Because of its design, it was the most analytically tractable of the experiments, though analysis is sometimes hampered by smaller than anticipated samples of recipients.

3. *The Housing Allowance Supply Experiment,* conducted by the Rand Corporation, collected data on some 50,000 direct cash assistance program applicants and recipients and 4,000 residential properties in two sites—South Bend, Indiana, and Green Bay, Wisconsin—from 1973

to 1979 (see Lowry, 1983). The focus of the Supply Experiment was evaluation of market supply response to increased housing demand. The increase in demand was to be created by offering direct cash assistance to all eligible households in the two sites—the only universal entitlement housing program ever run in the United States. Analysis was hampered by difficulties in estimating the change in housing demand among self-selected recipients and by the fact that the programs tested had a very small and rather program-specific effect on demand.

4. *The Section 8 Study*, conducted by Abt Associates, collected data in 1979 on the Section 8 New Construction and Existing Housing programs in a probability sample of sixteen Standard Metropolitan Statistical Areas (SMSAs), including about 12,000 applicants and recipients in 138 New Construction projects and 2,800 Existing Housing Program applicants and recipients (see Wallace and others, 1981). The Section 8 New Construction and Existing Housing programs replaced Section 23 in 1974. The New Construction program involves subsidies to private developers to build and operate low-income housing projects; the Existing Housing Program is a form of direct cash assistance, offering subsidies to low-income renters in the private market. The Section 8 study lacks any control group, although this is somewhat compensated for by preprogram information on recipients and nonrecipients.

5. *The Multifamily Development Cost Study*, conducted by Urban Systems, Research, and Engineering, examined the costs and project characteristics of a sample of about 800 multifamily projects developed between 1975 and 1979 under twelve different programs, including some effectively unsubsidized programs (see Schnare and others, 1982). The analysis focused on estimation of direct and indirect development costs and on comparison of costs with project quality. It was hampered by the need to rely heavily on construction cost indexes in order to adjust costs in different locations to allow comparisons across programs.

6. *The Housing Voucher Demonstration* now being conducted by Abt Associates is in the process of collecting data on some 10,000 applicants and recipients from the Section 8 Existing Housing Program in twenty PHAs. Interim findings suggest that the outcomes of the Section 8 Existing Housing Program may have changed substantially since the 1979 Section 8 study (see Kennedy and Finkel, 1987).

Four major findings emerge from these and other studies:

1. Construction programs are generally more expensive than programs that rely on the existing housing stock.

2. The higher costs of construction programs are only partly due to higher construction or operating costs than are found in the private market. In addition, the programs were frequently economically inefficient in the sense that when they were built existing units of the same quality could have been bought for less than the cost of new construction.

3. Direct cash assistance programs tend to reach households that already meet the program's housing requirements. They tend to relieve rent burdens rather than change housing, and the changes in housing that they do induce tend to be very specifically tied to the program housing standards.

4. Preliminary results from the Housing Voucher Demonstration suggest that the Section 8 Existing Housing Program outcomes may have changed materially over the last eight years—in particular, participation rates in 1986 may be much higher than in 1978, with much larger differences between program and preprogram rent levels.

Relative Costs of Direct Cash Assistance and Construction Programs

Housing programs vary in the housing provided, the costs involved, and the allocation of costs between tenant and program. The housing provided and the allocation of costs are potentially variable within each program type; they simply reflect current program rules regarding dwelling unit standards and subsidy schedules and could in principle be varied at will. Accordingly, a natural starting point is to compare the costs required under each program to produce a given "amount" of housing. This step is done by comparing costs to the equivalent rental value of similar units in the private market.

Probably the most exhaustive study of this sort was undertaken by Mayo, Mansfield, Warner, and Zwetchkenbaum (1980) in connection with the Housing Allowance Demand Experiment. The basic data available included physical inspections of samples of units in various housing programs in Pittsburgh and Phoenix, as well as units occupied by unsubsidized low-income renters in the private market, plus detailed information on the costs of each sampled housing program unit. Rental values were estimated by Merrill (1980) as a function of physical characteristics and location, as well as certain tenure conditions. Mayo, Mansfield, Warner, and Zwetchkenbaum estimated annualized costs for projects built in 1975 by regressing annualized per unit costs on estimated rental value (net of tenure factors), plus factors relating to program and year of construction. The results are shown in Table 1. The construction programs are markedly more expensive than the programs using the existing housing stock. Among those programs that use the existing housing stock, the original Section 23 program, in which PHAs leased units and sublet them to recipients, was more expensive than the Experimental Housing Allowance program, in which, like the current Section 8 (Existing) Program, recipients are responsible for finding units that meet program standards.

The major disadvantage of Mayo, Mansfield, Warner, and Zwetchkenbaum's findings is that they only refer to two cities—Pittsburgh and

Table 1. Estimates of Costs per Dollar of Rental Value
(for Units Built/Leased in 1975 in Pittsburgh and Phoenix)

	Annual Cost per Dollar of Rental Value[a] (standard deviation, sample size)
Construction Programs	
Public Housing (owned and operated by PHAs)	2.00[b] (0.13,466)
Section 236 (owned and operated by private developers under contract to HUD)	1.74[b] (0.17,368)
Existing Housing Programs	
Original Section 23 (units leased by PHAs and sublet to tenants)	1.45 (0.11,153)
Housing Allowance (units leased by recipients in the private market)[d]	1.12[c] (0.12,148)

[a] Figures are unweighted averages of estimates for Pittsburgh and Phoenix.
[b] Direct calculation for units constructed in 1970 to 1974 give somewhat lower estimates than the regression: Public Housing, 1.67; Section 236, 1.63.
[c] Excess costs for Housing Allowances are almost entirely estimated administrative costs.
[d] In the particular variant used here, households received subsidies equal to the difference between the estimated cost of modest, existing standard housing and 25 percent of net income if they occupied a unit that met program quality and occupancy standards.

Source: Mayo, Mansfield, Warner, and Zwetchkenbaum (1980) Part 2, Table 5-1 and p. 139. n. 2.

Phoenix. Indeed, though the pattern of results was the same in both sites, cost-value ratios for new construction programs were roughly 30 percent higher in Pittsburgh than in Phoenix. Unfortunately, information for other cities is hard to come by.

Although many earlier studies had established higher costs for construction programs, relatively few were able to estimate costs in terms of cost per dollar of rental value. HUD (U.S. Department of Housing and Urban Development, 1974, p. 126) estimated that Public Housing costs were roughly 23 percent higher than rental value for a sample of 356 families in six cities—much lower than Mayo, Mansfield, Warner, and Zwetchkenbaum's findings. Morrall and Olsen (1980) found that Section 23 Existing and New Construction programs in thirteen cities both had cost-value ratios only slightly greater than 1 and furthermore, that Pittsburgh was unusually expensive—raising doubts about the applicability of Mayo, Mansfield, Warner, and Zwetchkenbaum's estimates. Unfortunately, both these studies suffer from considerable measurement problems.

The great advantage that Mayo, Mansfield, Warner, and Zwetchkenbaum enjoyed was in having extensive observations on private, unsubsidized dwelling units with which to estimate market value. The method used by the U.S. Department of Housing and Urban Development (1974) to estimate market value is not clear but appears to have been based on U.S. Census data. If this were the case, it would mean that dwelling unit quality would be largely defined (beyond size) in terms of census tract and the absence of certain serious defects. This approach may tend to overvalue units substantially (see, for example, Wallace and others, 1981, pp. 326-327). Morrall and Olsen attempted to apply hedonic indices from a reference set of cities to other cities, adjusting for levels using either the Bureau of Labor Statistics (BLS) index or small numbers of unsubsidized units. The degree of error involved was not indicated.

At least two other studies have used direct estimates of equivalent rental value. Sumka and Stegman (1978) examined a sample of 600 private rental units and 173 Public Housing units in nonmetropolitan North Carolina and estimated a cost-value ratio of 2.10, somewhat higher than found by Mayo, Mansfield, Warner, and Zwetchkenbaum (1980). Wallace and others (1981) analyzed cost-value ratios for a national sample of Section 8 New Construction and Existing Housing units, again using estimated market rents based on observations of unsubsidized units in the same cities. The results, shown in Table 2, show considerably higher costs per unit value in the New Construction Program as compared with the Existing Housing Program, though figures in both programs are lower than those found by Mayo, Mansfield, Warner, and Zwetchkenbaum.

The difference between Wallace and others (1981) and Mayo, Mansfield, Warner, and Zwetchkenbaum (1980) is in part due to differences in the costs included. The analysis by Wallace and others did not include administrative costs nor various indirect subsidies in the form of various tax benefits included in Mayo's estimates. As shown in Table 2, omission of these costs would have reduced Mayo's estimates for Housing Allowances to less than 1 (that is, market value in excess of costs)—like the Wallace and others' finding for the Section 8 Existing Housing Program. Mayo's estimates for Section 236 new construction, however, would still have been substantially higher than the Wallace and others' estimates for the Section 8 New Construction Program.

Mayo's estimates are, of course, for only two sites, and the numbers sometimes differ considerably across sites, though the pattern across programs was always the same. In the case of Section 236 New Construction, Mayo's cost-value estimates (net of indirect costs omitted in Wallace and others) would have been 1.23 in Phoenix—almost exactly the same as Wallace and others' national estimate for Section 8 New Construction. Mayo's estimates in Pittsburgh were much higher.

Table 2. Estimate of Direct Costs per Dollar of Rental Value
for a National Sample of Section 8 New Construction
and Existing Housing Programs in 1979

	Direct Costs per Dollar of Rental Value (standard deviation, sample size)	Comparable Costs per Dollar Figures from Mayo, Mansfield, Warner, and Zwetchkenbaum (1980)
Section 8 New Construction	1.24[a] (0.02,186)	1.49[b] (0.17) (Section 236 New Construction)
Section 8 Existing Housing	0.91[a] (0.01,276)	0.97[c] (0.12) (housing allowances)

[a]Standard errors are upper bounds for the asymptotic approximation for the ratio of estimated average costs and average values.
[b]This figure gives Mayo's Section 236 Estimated Cost per Dollar Value for Section 236 New Construction only and reducing costs by indirect costs not included in Wallace and others, 1981 (FHA Insurance, GNMA Tandem, foregone local property taxes, foregone federal taxes due to accelerated depreciation, and HUD Area and Central Office Administration). See Mayo, pp. 61, 122, 168.
[c]This represents the figure for Housing Allowances in Table 1, net of estimated administrative costs. See Mayo, Mansfield, Warner, and Zwetchkenbaum, 1980, p. 137.
Source: Wallace and others, 1981, pp. 222, 336.

Variation over time and place in cost-value ratios for construction programs would not surprise Mayo, Mansfield, Warner, and Zwetchkenbaum (1980) and indeed this is a key point in their analysis. They argue that evidence suggests that only part of the inefficiency found in construction programs is the sort of technical inefficiency (in the sense of excessive construction or operating costs) that is likely to persist consistently over time and place. They suggest that a major element was simple economic inefficiency—that much of the construction undertaken was inefficient not because costs were higher than in the private market, but because it simply did not pay to construct rental housing at the time. In support, Mayo, Mansfield, Warner, and Zwetchkenbaum present evidence that inefficiency increased over time, paralleling a rapid rise in construction costs relative to rents.

Some support for this hypothesis is also found in a study by Schnare and others (1982) that compared development costs for Section 8, Public Housing, and Section 236 with those of similar unsubsidized units. They found that development costs for Section 236 and Section 8 (Substantial Rehabilitation) were essentially the same (±1 percent) as those for similar unsubsidized units. Development costs in Section 8 (New Construction) and Public Housing were significantly higher, but only by 8.6 and 33.2 percent, respectively—not nearly enough to account for observed cost-value ratios.

Schnare and others (1982) analyze construction cost differentials by regressing costs on project characteristics and program. Their results do not appear to depend heavily on the regression specification. The cost figures were adjusted for differences in time and place using the Dodge Construction Index and a land cost index developed by Schnare and others. Unfortunately, examination of adjusted and unadjusted costs (Schnare and others, Appendixes B and C) suggests that the findings of program differences depend heavily on these adjustments.

Mayo, Mansfield, Warner, and Zwetchkenbaum's (1980) hypothesis, if correct, has three important implications. First, it suggests that, however valuable they may be, attempts to improve the efficiency of construction programs are not likely to reduce costs enough to overcome the underlying difference in market prices. Second, given a rapid enough inflation in rents relative to construction costs and interest rates, construction programs could become a cheaper means of providing low-income housing than direct cash assistance. Indeed, this relationship could hold true even if public construction were less efficient than private construction. Finally, the hypothesis suggests that the problem is how units are obtained, not whether they are owned or leased. In principle, the government might be able to purchase existing units for public housing at no greater (eventual) cost than leasing them would entail. Equally important, if most of the excess costs of construction programs arise at the construction stage, only modest savings would be realized from the sale of already built units and conversion of subsidies to direct cash assistance.

The Effects of Direct Cash Assistance

The most common forms of direct cash assistance involve two elements: (1) a payment determined by income, household size, and local housing costs, and (2) requirements that the applicant's housing must meet in order to qualify for payments. The housing requirements for direct cash assistance distinguish it from a simple cash transfer. The key findings are that these requirements both substantially restrict participation and often have highly specific program effects.

The Housing Allowance Demand Experiment tested two sorts of housing requirements—a minimum standards requirement, which specified various physical standards (including minimum bedroom size), and a minimum rent requirement, which simply set a floor on the acceptable unit rent. The Demand Experiment also tested a rent rebate program (see Friedman and Weinberg, 1980a). Because we had control households, we were able to analyze participation in terms of the probability of meeting housing requirements in the absence of the program. Indeed, Kennedy and MacMillan found this was the only determinant of participation. Once households enrolled, they participated if they would normally meet requirements without the program or if the allowance payment offered them was large enough to induce them to meet requirements. Demographic characteristics, housing, and willingness to move had no effect on participation except as they affected either the normal propensity to occupy required housing or the payment level (Kennedy and MacMillan, 1980, chapter 4). (This is a slight overstatement, however. As discussed later, some households chose not to enroll at all. In general, enrollment rates varied with payments and ran at 85 to 90 percent once payments exceeded $30 per month. There were, however, various demographic differences in acceptance, idiosyncratic to each site, and apparently reflecting a general willingness to participate in any sort of program. See Kennedy and MacMillan, 1980, chapter 2.)

The surprising finding was how low participation rates were among households that would not normally have met requirements. Average participation rates in the two Demand Experiment sites varied considerably across the three housing requirements (the rates were 38, 45, and 60 percent for minimum standards, a high minimum rent, and a low minimum rent, respectively). This variation was almost entirely due to differences in the rate at which households would normally have met the different housing requirements in the absence of the program. In each case, 78 percent of households that would normally meet requirements on their own participated in the program. Estimated participation rates among those that would not normally meet requirements, however, were uniformly much lower—between 19 and 23 percent.

Participation rates can be increased by increasing payments. Average payments offered to households in the minimum standards plans were close to 20 percent of income. Doubling these payments was estimated to increase participation rates from 38 percent (19 percent for those that would not normally meet requirements) to 56 percent (45 percent for those that would not normally meet requirements). (See Kennedy, 1980, p. 169.)

Evidence from the Supply Experiment modifies these findings in two ways. First, high failure rates can be consistent with high participation rates if households can easily repair their units to meet requirements. The Supply Experiment used a direct cash assistance program with minimum standards; however, the standards were less stringent than those used in the Demand Experiment in two ways: (1) more households met the standards to begin with, and (2) many of the failures involved deficiencies that were relatively easy to repair. The effect of this difference can be seen by comparing participation rates for minimum standards enrollees in the Demand Experiment with those of similar households in the Supply Experiment. Now the base is not all eligible households (as in the earlier discussion), but people who actually apply for the program. Among these, the participation rate in the Supply Experiment was 88 percent, as compared to 47 percent for minimum standards enrollees in the Demand Experiment. The higher rate for the Supply Experiment is entirely attributable to (1) a higher percentage of applicants who already lived in housing that met program requirements (48 versus 17 percent) and (2) among these not living in housing that already met program requirements, to a much higher percentage able to repair their preprogram units to qualify (58 versus 17 percent). Among households that had to move or repair their units to correct deficiencies, the percentage moving to program acceptable units was almost identical in the two experiments (19 versus 20 percent). (See Kennedy and MacMillan, 1983, p. 103; and Lowry, 1983, pp. 113-114.)

Second, analyses of the Supply Experiment and the Administrative Agency Experiment (AAE) suggest that operating programs will have lower participation rates among all eligible households than those found in the Demand Experiment. Two factors are involved. To begin with, the Demand Experiment was based on a sample of eligible households that were individually approached and offered enrollment. This sample represents a more extensive outreach than seems conceivable for any operating program. In the Supply Experiment, with very extensive outreach, 85 percent of the eligible population knew about the program after three years (Lowry, 1983, p. 134). Of these households, about 76 percent chose to enroll in the program—very similar to the 78 percent acceptance rate in the Demand Experiment. In contrast, in the one AAE site where data were collected on program awareness, less than 25 percent of eligibles were aware of the program, and of these well under 40 percent applied for enrollment (Hamilton, 1979, p. 28). Furthermore, the AAE analysis found evidence that reaching outside of the existing social service network frequently requires special efforts by PHAs.

The other factor reducing participation is simply dynamics. The participation rates just presented refer to the probability that households ever become recipients. But participation takes time, and the eligible population is constantly reformed. Analysis of the Supply Experiment found that somewhat less than one-third of the eligible population turned over each year. Given enrollment delays, this turnover reduced participation as a percentage of the current eligible population by a factor of 10 to 15 percent (Lowry, 1983, pp. 95, 125).

The importance of these findings is twofold. First, of course, they directly mean that the imposition of housing requirements will cut off most households that would not normally meet these requirements (or cannot easily meet them by minor repairs) from participating in the program. In terms of demographic groups, housing requirements in the

Demand Experiment significantly reduced participation among minorities, large households, and the very poor (Kennedy, 1980, p. 134).

In addition, however, housing requirements materially affect the impact of the program on recipient housing. For households that would normally meet housing requirements on their own, the cash assistance subsidy is like any other income transfer, and results in only modest changes in housing. Only households that are induced by the program to meet requirements are forced to change their housing. Thus, there is a direct tradeoff between housing change and participation; the more stringent the requirements, the greater the average change among recipients, but the lower the participation rate.

Furthermore, effects are sometimes remarkably specific to the exact requirements imposed. Friedman and Weinberg found, for example, that when the impact of direct cash assistance with a minimum standards requirement was measured in terms of an alternative set of standards to those actually used in the minimum standard requirement, estimated impact was less than half the impact measured in terms of meeting the actual requirements. Nor did programs with minimum rent requirements have any significant effect in terms of meeting the minimum standards requirement (Friedman and Weinberg, 1980b, pp. 19, 27, 60). Likewise, minimum standards requirements had much more modest effects on housing expenditures than minimum rent requirements. At the same time, a substantial portion of the expenditure increase obtained under minimum rent requirements was just that—expenditure increase without any corresponding increase in real housing.

Friedman and Weinberg estimated both impacts on expenditures and impacts on real housing, based on comparison of randomly assigned control and treatment groups, taking account of participant self-selection. Real housing change was estimated in terms of the estimated market value of the units, based on the regressions of pre-enrollment and control household rents on various units and locational characteristic by Merrill (1980). They found that minimum standard requirements had roughly the same impact as the low minimum rent requirements in terms of expenditure change (10.3 and 9.3 percent increases, respectively), but considerably less than the high minimum rent requirement (an 18.5 percent increase). All three programs had much smaller changes in terms of housing services, with no significant difference across the three programs. (The estimated effect on housing services were increases of 6.7, 5.5, and 9.5 percent, respectively.)

The role of housing requirements in allocating effects across households can be indicated by comparing effects for households that already met requirements when they enrolled (most of whom would have continued to meet them) and those that only met requirements after enrollment (a substantial fraction of whom were induced to meet the requirements).

Considering only households that moved at some point during the experiment (those that changed their housing), households that already met requirements at enrollment showed no significant impact on either housing expenditures or housing services (estimated impacts were 1.4 and 0.9 percent, respectively). Moving households that met requirements after enrollment, however, were estimated to have been induced to increase expenditures by 22.3 percent and services by 9.9 percent (both statistically significant). (See Friedman and Weinberg, 1980b, Tables 7-13 to 7-15, 7-21 to 7-23.)

Finally, when Friedman and Weinberg compared estimated effects on housing allowance recipients with households receiving similar payments without housing requirements, they found that only the high minimum rent requirement produced any significantly higher effects on housing expenditures or services, and then only with respect to expenditures. It should be emphasized, however, that the allowance programs did have significant effects in terms of inducing households to meet the various housing requirements. In general, unconstrained payments had no effect in terms of meeting minimum standards requirements. Such payments did tend to increase the proportion of households meeting minimum rent requirements, but by substantially less than the actual imposition of requirements. The fact is that the effects of requirements were both highly specific to the requirement and involved the relatively small percentage of recipients that were actually induced to meet the requirements by the program. (See Friedman and Weinberg, 1980b, Tables 5-9, 5-14, and IX-42 to IX-44, and pp. A-119, A-123, A-125.)

It should be noted that the concentration of housing change among households that were induced by the program to meet housing requirements was quite intentional. In effect, the program allows recipients who are already in acceptable housing to use the program assistance to reduce their high rent burdens while requiring households in unacceptable housing to use at least part of the assistance to improve their housing. What was unexpected was the low participation rate among households in unacceptable housing and the specificity of the housing change for those that did participate.

Some Recent Results

Analysis of the Section 8 Existing Housing Program in 1979 by Wallace and others (1981) and by Kennedy and Wallace (1983) confirmed the findings of the Housing Allowance Experiments with respect to the participation rates and program impact. However, recent early findings from the Housing Voucher Demonstration look markedly different. The Section 8 study analyzed by Wallace and others and by Kennedy and Wallace was based on data for the Section 8 New Construction and Existing Housing programs in 1979 in a probability sample of 16 SMSAs. The Housing Voucher Demonstration, now underway, is intended to compare two forms of direct cash assistance, one of which is the same Section 8 Existing Housing Program that was analyzed in the 1979 Section 8 study. Table 3 presents success rates and change in average expenditures found in the Demand Experiment for the minimum standards program and in the 1979 Section 8 Study and the current Housing Voucher Demonstration for the Section 8 Existing Housing Certificate Program.

The 1979 Section 8 Existing Housing Program had almost the same overall participation rate as the similar program tested in the Demand Experiment; a much lower percentage of Section 8 applicants were able to qualify in their pre-enrollment unit without moving, but a much larger percentage qualified by moving. The two programs had similar ratios of program to preprogram rents. However, the 1979 Section 8 Existing Housing Program showed very little change in average housing services. By 1986, however, the participation rate in the Section 8 Existing Housing Program was much higher than in 1979, primarily due to a very substantial increase in the percent of applicant households that qualified by moving. Furthermore, the percentage increase in average rents was very much larger—51 percent as compared with 19 percent in

Table 3. Comparison of Findings from the Demand Experiment, the 1979 Section 8 Study, and the 1986 Housing Voucher Demonstration

Participation Rate Among Applicants	Demand Experiment (minimum standards)	Section 8 Existing Housing Certificate Program 1979	Section 8 Existing Housing Certificate Program 1986
Overall	47%	46%	60%
Percent of applicants that qualify without moving	31%	20%[a]	23%
Percent of applicants that qualify by moving	17%	26%[a]	37%
Ratio of average program rent to average preprogram rent	1.19[b]	1.19[b]	1.51[b]
Ratio of average program housing services to average preprogram housing services	1.10	1.02	n.a.

[a]Figures may not be exact. See Kennedy and Finkel, 1987, Appendix II, for details of derivation.
[b]Rent figures refer to contract rent for 1986 and to gross rent (contract rent plus allowances for utilities not included in the rent) for the Demand Experiment and the 1979 Section 8 data. Definitions may not be completely comparable across the three studies.

Sources: Kennedy and Finkel, 1987, pp. 35, 51; Wallace and others, 1981, p. 317.

the 1979 study. No information is yet available on change in housing services.

These numbers need to be viewed with a considerable degree of caution. The data for 1986 are early tabulations of results and have not been analyzed in any detail. The higher participation rates in 1986 may represent a genuine shift in program success rates; in particular, it seems possible that as the program has matured, it has become much easier for applicants to find housing that meets program requirements simply because more landlords are involved in the program. Yet higher observed participation rates might also be due to other factors such as generally looser rental markets, more effective self-selection by applicants, or some undetected gradual relaxation in the enforcement of housing standards. Similarly, the dramatic difference in the ratio of average program to average preprogram rents may reflect either a real change in housing impact or a change in background trends. Indeed, it is not at all clear from the published reports that the definitions of expenditures were the same in the 1979 and 1986 analyses. Furthermore, the numbers may be substantially affected by the presence and treatment of subunits—recipients that were previously part of a larger household and may have been paying very little or nothing for rent. Even so, the preliminary results from the Housing Voucher Demonstration do raise the possibility that direct cash assistance may have become markedly more effective over time.

Reprise

We know that construction programs are relatively expensive. Furthermore, some of this is apparently technical inefficiency in the sense of higher than necessary construction and operating costs, while some is simply a mistaken decision to build rather than buy. However, it appears that programs using the existing housing stock do not generally reach those in the worst housing. Furthermore, direct cash assistance programs of the sort currently in use produce large housing changes only among households that are induced to meet housing requirements. Therefore the programs have relatively small effects on overall recipient housing; most of the assistance goes to reducing rent burdens.

These findings suggest three areas for further investigation. First, can we better define the target population—those whom we want to reach with housing assistance? We simply do not have a very good characterization of poverty and particularly of housing inadequacy. If the issue is rent burden, then we are substantially restricting relief with irrelevant housing standards. If the issue is (also) housing quality and availability, then we need to examine the incidence of inadequate housing per se.

Budding (1980), for example, analyzing the detailed data on housing quality and rents in the Demand Experiment, found a much higher incidence of inadequate housing than is indicated by generally available measures. Incidence was strongly related to poverty, declining approximately linearly from 75 percent among households with incomes of less than half the poverty level to 21 percent among households with incomes greater than twice the poverty level (see Kennedy, 1980, p. 35). The inclusion of rent burden in terms of rents greater than a fixed percent of income led to a much flatter incidence profile, with the incidence running from 90 percent among households with incomes of less than half the poverty level to 65 percent among households with incomes greater than twice the poverty level. Furthermore, the drop in incidence was very small until household incomes exceeded 1.75 times the poverty level (Kennedy, 1980, p. 33). As Budding pointed out, however, setting rent burden limits in terms of a fixed percent of income is highly arbitrary. He suggested instead that rent burden be classified as insupportable if income after rent was less than poverty-level income net of poverty-level housing costs. Under this definition, the incidence of housing deprivation is much more heavily concentrated among the poor.

Second, is there a role for the Public Housing Authority in providing improved access to housing for eligible families that will not succeed in participating in direct cash assistance programs? We simply do not have an adequate understanding of the barriers to participation in direct cash assistance programs or the extent to which these can be offset by the availability of units that are specifically earmarked for low-income housing. A first step here would be to examine profiles of Section 8 Existing Housing and New Construction program participants, with special attention to previous housing conditions. This examination would also allow us to develop better estimates of construction program impact on housing.

Third, are there program mechanisms that would accomplish this role without incurring the excess costs found for current construction programs? Two issues are involved here. One is under what circumstances, if any, we need to intervene directly to increase the supply of low-income housing. Because the direct cash assistance program tested in the Supply Experiment resulted in only very marginal changes in demand, we still have little information on the rapidity of market construction response. The second issue concerns possible mechanisms. We have little information on the extent of operating inefficiencies in either public housing or privately managed new construction programs such as Section 236 or Section 8 New Construction. Equally important, Schnare and others (1982) found no excess development costs for Section 236 and only modest ones for Section 8. The fact is that HUD has never tried to run a Section 8 New Construction Program offering the same subsidy levels as in the Section 8

Existing Housing Program. Such a policy would in theory elicit new construction only when the market indicated a need for increased supply, thus avoiding the large economic inefficiencies found by Mayo, Mansfield, Warner, and Zwetchkenbaum (1980). Nor has HUD apparently explored the possibility of providing earmarked units through purchase of existing buildings or through allowing private owners to convert entire buildings to Section 8. (Although Mayo's findings with respect to Section 23 in Pittsburgh and Phoenix would at least raise some questions about the government's bargaining ability. Again, the mechanism might be to use the payments set for the Section 8 Existing Housing Program.)

Finally, the early results from the Housing Voucher Demonstration raise a fourth important set of issues: Have the impacts of the Section 8 Existing Housing Program in fact changed materially over time, and if so, why? This issue arises more generally. Public housing, for example, appears to be much less successful today than it was in the 1930s and 1940s. Our evaluations of programs are frequently based on analysis of one or two years. If programs really evolve over time, such analyses can be substantially misleading. We need to understand this evolutionary process better. At the very least, it suggests a need for ongoing operating program data collection and regular publication of usable summary statistics to track key outcomes and alert policymakers to possible changes in program performance.

References

Budding, D. W. *Housing Deprivation Among Enrollees in the Housing Allowance Demand Experiment.* Cambridge, Mass.: Abt Associates, 1980.
Friedman, J., and Weinberg, D. H. *The Demand for Rental Housing: Evidence from a Percent of Rent Housing Allowance.* Cambridge, Mass.: Abt Associates, 1980a.
Friedman, J., and Weinberg, D. H. *Housing Consumption Under a Constrained Income Transfer: Evidence from a Housing Gap Housing Allowance.* Cambridge, Mass.: Abt Associates, 1980b.
Hamilton, W. L. *A Social Experiment in Program Administration: The Housing Allowance Administrative Agency Experiment.* Cambridge, Mass.: Abt Books, 1979.
Kennedy, S. D. *The Final Report of the Housing Allowance Demand Experiment.* Cambridge, Mass.: Abt Associates, 1980.
Kennedy, S. D., and Finkel, M. *Report of First-Year Findings for the Freestanding Housing Voucher Demonstration.* Cambridge, Mass.: Abt Associates, 1987.
Kennedy, S. D., Kumar, T. K., and Weisbrod, G. *Participation Under a Housing Gap Form of Housing Allowance.* Cambridge, Mass.: Abt Associates, 1980.
Kennedy, S. D., and MacMillan, J. E. *Participation Under Alternative Housing Allowance Programs: Evidence from the Housing Allowance Demand Experiment.* Cambridge, Mass.: Abt Associates, 1980.
Kennedy, S. D., and MacMillan, J. E. "Participation Under Random Assignment." In J. Friedman and D. H. Weinberg (eds.), *The Great Housing Experiment.* Newbury Park, Calif.: Sage, 1983.

Kennedy, S. D., and Merrill, S. R. "The Use of Hedonic Indices to Distinguish Changes in Housing and Housing Expenditures: Evidence from the Housing Allowance Demand Experiment." Paper presented at the Research Conference on the Housing Choices of Low-Income Families, Washington, D.C., Mar. 1979.

Kennedy, S. D., and Wallace, J. E. *An Evaluation of Success Rates in Housing Assistance Programs Using the Existing Housing Stock.* Cambridge, Mass.: Abt Associates, 1983.

Lowry, I. S. *Experimenting with Housing Allowances: The Final Report of the Housing Assistance Supply Experiment.* Cambridge, Mass.: Oelgeschlager, Gunn, and Hain, 1983.

Mayo, S. K., Mansfield, S., Warner, D., and Zwetchkenbaum, R. *Housing Allowances and Other Rental Housing Assistance Programs—A Comparison Based on the Housing Allowance Demand Experiment. Part 1: Participation, Housing Consumption, Location, and Satisfaction. Part 2: Costs and Efficiency.* Cambridge, Mass.: Abt Associates, 1980.

Merrill, S. R. *Hedonic Indices as a Measure of Housing Quality.* Cambridge, Mass.: Abt Associates, 1980.

Morrall, J. F., and Olsen, E. O. "The Cost-Effectiveness of Leased Public Housing." *Policy Analysis,* Spring 1980, pp. 151-170.

Schnare, A. B., Moss, W. B., Pedone, C. I., Heintz, K. G., and Wiley, B. P. *The Costs of HUD Multifamily Housing Programs: An Analysis of Development, Financing, and Subsidy Expenditures.* Cambridge, Mass.: Urban Systems, Research, and Engineering, 1982.

Sumka, H. J., and Stegman, M. A. "An Economic Analysis of Public Housing in Small Cities." *Journal of Regional Science,* 1978, *18* (3), 395-410.

U.S. Department of Housing and Urban Development. *Housing in the Seventies: A Report of the National Policy Review.* Washington, D.C.: U.S. Department of Housing and Urban Development, 1974.

Wallace, J. E., Bloom, S. P., Holshouser, W. L., Mansfield, S., and Weinberg, D. H. *Participation and Benefits in the Urban Section 8 Program: New Construction and Existing Housing.* Cambridge, Mass.: Abt Associates, 1981.

Stephen D. Kennedy is a senior economist at Abt Associates, Inc., Cambridge, Massachusetts. Dr. Kennedy was project director for the Housing Demand Experiment and is an expert on housing programs and social experiments.

Fair housing audits, an innovative quasi-experimental technique, have made it possible to study the incidence and intensity of housing discrimination faced by minority families. Results from the application of this technique indicate that groups such as black, Hispanic, and Asian Americans face substantial discrimination in terms of the number, types, and location of housing units they are shown by realtors.

Examining Racial Discrimination with Fair Housing Audits

John Yinger

Racial discrimination in housing exists whenever a member of a racial minority is denied access to available housing or offered housing on less favorable terms than whites simply because of his or her minority status. This type of discrimination was prohibited by the Civil Rights Act of 1968, but until recently researchers have not been able to determine whether it persists despite this prohibition.

A fair housing audit is a quasi-experimental survey technique that allows a researcher to measure racial discrimination in housing through direct observation. Preaudit research measured housing discrimination indirectly by determining whether urban residential structure reflected the theoretically derived effects of discrimination, such as higher prices in largely black areas and more centralized patterns of black residence than of white residence. This indirect approach is difficult to implement, and studies without careful theoretical formulations and extensive controls for nonracial determinants of urban structure do not yield compelling results. (For a review of the studies employing this indirect approach, see Yinger, 1979.) By enabling direct observation, fair housing audits represent a major methodological advance in the study of racial discrimination in housing.

Fair housing audits were developed by community-based fair housing groups as a way to investigate complaints by minority housing seekers who thought they had encountered discrimination. The first research use of these audits in the United States was the pioneer study by Wienk, Reid, Simonson, and Eggers (1979). (An earlier study, McIntosh and Smith, 1974, employed this technique in Great Britain.) Since then, four more large studies, all of which yield compelling results, along with several small ones, have been carried out. This chapter reviews what we have learned from these studies. The first section explains the audit technique; the second section describes the audit studies and summarizes their key results.

The Audit Technique

A fair housing audit is a controlled investigation into the marketing practices of a housing agent, such as a landlord or real estate broker. An individual from the white majority and an individual from a minority group are carefully matched (through selection, assignment, and training) according to their family and economic characteristics. The two teammates then visit the agent within a short time of each other to inquire about housing. Both auditors are instructed to learn about and visit as many housing units as possible, but they do not attempt to complete a rental or sales transaction.

An audit study is a set of audits conducted on a random sample of the advertised housing units in a given housing market. (For more on the issue of sampling, see Wienk, Reid, Simonson, and Eggers, 1979; Feins and others, 1981; or Yinger, 1984.) The universe of advertised units is identified from newspaper ads. Most studies are based on a simple random sample of advertised units, although a few authors assume that ads for apartment buildings represent more than one available unit and alter their sampling plan accordingly.

Discrimination is the average difference in the treatment of minority and majority auditors. Thus, an audit study yields an estimate of discrimination in the marketing of advertised housing units in a given housing market. Other techniques must be used to measure discrimination in other stages of a housing transaction, such as in credit checks or in the granting of mortgages, and in housing that is not advertised. (Several studies have employed regression techniques to study discrimination in mortgage lending. See, for example, Schafer and Ladd, 1981.)

The Audit Design. The design of a fair housing audit has evolved to ensure against threats to internal validity. Many variables other than minority status influence the treatment an auditor receives; the audit design assures that these variables do not influence the difference in teammates' treatments. Three types of variables must be considered: the order in which teammates visit a housing agent; the circumstances of the audit, including conditions in the housing market at the time of the audit and the characteristics of the housing agent; and the characteristics of the auditor.

By necessity, one teammate must go first and may, for that reason, be treated differently from his or her teammate. A rental agent may think, for example, that the first auditor is likely to rent the one available apartment and therefore may try to discourage the second auditor. Random assignment of order, as implemented by Feins, Bratt, and Hollister (1981) and by Holshouser (1984) ensures that order does not systematically influence the difference in teammates' treatment. Feins, Bratt, and Hollister discovered that order does not have a significant effect on treatment, so the nonrandom order probably is not a problem in other studies.

Teammates cannot visit an agent at the same time, but they do visit the same agent in short succession, typically within one hour of each other. Thus, they encounter the same agency characteristics and the same housing market conditions. Because these factors are the same for teammates, they cannot influence the difference in teammates' treatment.

Although teammates visit the same agency, they may encounter different agents. Suppose minority auditors are systematically assigned to "stingier" agents and therefore learn about fewer housing units. In this case, the assignment process is simply the method by which the agency discriminates and the resulting difference in teammates' treatment is a legitimate measure of discrimination. However, the assignment of an agent to a customer may be a random process or may depend on customer characteristics other than minority status. In either case, variation in treatment across agents is not correlated with differences in treatment between teammates.

Finally, the way an agent treats his or her customers (or auditors) may depend on their age, income, and family characteristics. To ensure that these characteristics do not lead to differences in teammates' treatment, an audit matches teammates on these characteristics. Matching is achieved in three ways. First, the selection process avoids people with unusual personalities and pairs teammates with the same indelible characteristics, such as age and sex. Second, auditors are assigned income and family characteristics for the purpose of each audit, and teammates are always given similar assignments. Third, all auditors are given the same training so that their behavior in the audit setting does not elicit unusual treatment.

An audit is not a fully experimental method, however. One cannot, after all, randomly assign the key characteristic, namely minority status. Consequently, one cannot totally eliminate the possibility that teammates differ on some characteristic that influences their treatment. Nevertheless, careful pairing, role assignment, and training can eliminate major differences in teammate characteristics. It seems reasonable to conclude that any differences in teammates' treatment—other than differences due to minority status—are due to random differences between teammates or between the circumstances teammates encounter and therefore do not threaten the internal validity of inferences about discrimination. Because auditors must be trained and matched, however, the results of an audit study cannot be generalized to minority group members who are very different from the auditors.

Measuring the Level of Discrimination. The level of discrimination is the extent to which minority auditors are treated less favorably than majority auditors. One can measure the level of discrimination with a standard difference-of-means test. Let A stand for an action taken by a housing agent toward an auditor, such as the number of apartments the auditor is invited to inspect, and suppose a higher value of A implies more favorable treatment. Then the difference in the mean treatment of majority and minority auditors, calculated over the N audits in the sample, measures the level of discrimination. The t-test for this difference in the mean treatment is a test of the hypothesis that discrimination exists.

Although a *standard* difference-of-means test correctly estimates the level of discrimination, it does not yield the correct standard error for this estimate. In fact, the standard test systematically overstates this standard error and therefore could lead researchers or enforcement officials to conclude that discrimination does not exist when in fact it does. This problem arises because, thanks largely to the audit design, the treatment encountered by two teammates is not independent. Characteristics shared by two teammates have the same effect on the treatment of both. Fortunately, however, this problem can easily be corrected by using a *paired* difference-of-means test, which yields the same estimate of the level of discrimination as the standard test but which also yields the correct standard error.

Measuring the Probability of Discrimination. Another way to measure discrimination with a fair housing audit is to determine the probability that a minority housing seeker will encounter discriminatory treatment when he or she visits a housing agent. This probability is measured by the proportion of the audits in which the majority auditor was treated more favorably than the minority auditor.

Most studies focus on the net probability of encountering discrimination, which is the proportion of audits in which the majority auditor was favored minus the proportion of audits in which the minority auditor was favored. This net probability also can be examined with a difference-of-means test. Let D_{ai} indicate whether Auditor i encounters discrimination in Audit a; that is, let D_{ai} equal 1 if that auditor is treated less favorably than his or her teammate on a particular action and let it equal 0 (zero) otherwise. Then the mean value of D_{ai} for minority auditors is the gross probability that minorities will encounter discrimination, and the difference in the mean values of D_{ai} for minority and majority auditors is the net probability of discrimination against minorities.

A paired difference-of-means test is needed to obtain the correct standard error for an estimated net probability of discrimination. Unfavorable treatment for one teammate implies favorable treatment for his or her teammate, so the correlation between teammates is exactly -1 (negative one). With some neutral audits, which are audits in which neither teammate is favored, this correlation is still negative, but is closer to zero. In studying the probability of discrimination, therefore, a standard difference-of-means test yields standard errors that are biased downward and may lead a researcher to conclude that the net probability of discrimination is significant when in fact it is not. A paired difference-of-means test eliminates this problem. Wienk, Reid, Simonson, and Eggers (1979) employ a nonparametric test, namely the sign test, instead of a t-test. This approach yields results that are similar to a paired difference-of-means test. In Yinger (1984), I argue that, particularly for large samples, a sign test is less appropriate for audit data than is a t-test.

One could argue that net discrimination underestimates the probability that a minority will encounter discrimination. Consider an agent who tries to discriminate but whose actions are influenced by random factors, such as the number of apartments he or she has available or how close it is to lunch time. This agent will favor the minority auditor only when random factors more than offset his or her attempts to discriminate. When random factors favor the majority auditor, however, they increase the *severity* of discrimination against the minority auditor but have no effect on the *probability* of discrimination. As a result, it makes no sense to net out minority-favored audits. In fact, net discrimination is the right measure only if an agent is trying to be neutral but, for random reasons, sometimes favors the minority auditor and sometimes favors the majority auditor. As we will see, existing studies rule out this case; majority auditors are favored far more often than minority auditors. Nevertheless, gross discrimination may reflect some random unfavorable treatment. Under these circumstances, it seems reasonable to consider net discrimination to be a lower bound and gross discrimination to be an upper bound on the probability that a minority person will encounter discrimination. In Yinger (1984), I argue that one can employ information about the characteristics of the auditor, agent, and the audit to estimate the systematic component of discrimination. My preliminary application of this technique indicates that the probability of encountering systematic discrimination is closer to the gross measures described in the text than it is to the net measures.

A second complication, also identified by Wienk, Reid, Simonson, and Eggers (1979) is that one may want to know the probability of discrimination in a set of actions instead of in a single action. Wienk and others introduce two ways to calculate the probability of discrimination in a category of actions, such as the actions that affect housing availability. The first way is to say that an audit is neutral if each teammate was favored on at least one action and that an auditor was favored overall if he or she was favored on at least one action and his or her teammate was favored on none. This approach is somewhat extreme because an audit in which one auditor is favored on five out of six items and the other auditor is favored on the sixth, is rated as neutral. Thus, the second way is to say that the auditor favored on the most actions is favored overall. Several of the studies that have followed Wienk, Reid, Simonson, and Eggers (1979) also employ these two approaches.

What Have We Learned About Discrimination from Audit Studies?

The Studies. Five recent, large audit studies are described in Table 1. All five are high-quality studies that pay careful attention to sampling, data collection, management, and study design. These studies were all carried out between 1977 and 1983 and cover a wide range of U.S. cities. Four of the studies examine discrimination against blacks, three examine discrimination against Hispanics, and one examines discrimination against Southeast Asians. Although they address somewhat different questions about discrimination, all five studies employ similar survey forms and estimate the level and/or the probability of discrimination. One other study, Pearce (1979), collected more specialized audit data, and several studies—including Newberger (1981), Simonson and Wienk (1984), and Yinger (1986)—have asked further questions about discrimination using data from one of the studies in Table 1. Numerous small audit studies, some of which are reviewed in Newberger (1984) or in Yinger (1984), also have been carried out.

Lessons from Audit Studies. The following discussion summarizes the major lessons learned from the studies listed above.

Lesson 1. The level of discrimination is very high in many cities. Three studies estimate the level of discrimination, as defined in the first section of this chapter. Table 2 summarizes the results of these studies for three measures of housing availability: the number of units discussed as serious possibilities, the number of units the auditor was invited to inspect, and the number of units the auditor actually inspected.

Feins, Bratt, and Hollister (1981) uncovered high levels of discrimination in Boston for all three housing availability measures. For example, black auditors were invited to inspect 0.94 units on average compared

Table 1. Description of Five Audit Studies

Study	City	Year	Minority Group	Number of Audits
Wienk, Reid, Simonson, and Eggers (1979)	40 SMSAs	1977	Black renters Black owners	1,609 1,655
Hakken (1979)	Dallas	1978	Dark-skinned Hispanic renters Light-skinned Hispanic renters	73 75
Feins, Bratt, and Hollister (1981)	Boston	1981	Black renters Black owners	156 118
James, McCummings, and Tynan (1983)	Denver	1982	Hispanic renters Black renters Hispanic owners Black owners	62 70 72 49
Holshouser (1984)	Boston	1983	Black renters Hispanic renters Southeast Asian renters Black owners Hispanic owners	23 12 18 38 25

to 1.70 units for whites. This result implies that a black seeker of housing would have to visit nine agents to receive as many invitations as whites receive from five agents. The Holshouser study, which was carried out in different parts of Boston than the earlier Feins, Bratt, and Hollister study, found continuing high levels of discrimination against blacks as well as high levels of discrimination against Hispanics and Asian Americans. Finally, James, McCummings, and Tynan (1983) discovered widespread, but not universal, discrimination in Denver. Hispanic owners and black renters faced high levels of discrimination on all three measures, whereas Hispanic renters and black owners faced high levels of discrimination in some parts of the urban area. To be specific, black owners faced discrimination in Anglo suburbs and Hispanic renters faced discrimination in Hispanic sections of Denver.

Most of these estimates of the discrimination level are statistically significant at the 95 percent level. Furthermore, James, McCummings, and Tynan (1983) employed a standard difference-of-means test instead of the appropriate paired test, so some of the results they report as insignificant may in fact be significant.

Lesson 2. The probability of encountering discrimination is very high in many cities. Four studies estimate the probability of encountering discrimination. Their findings are summarized in Table 3. Many of the

Table 2. Estimates of the Level of Discrimination
in Housing Availability (number of housing units)

Number of Sample	Measure of Housing Availability[a]			
	Possibilities	Invited to See	Inspected	Audits
Boston, 1981[b]				
Black renters	0.641	0.764	0.537	156
Black owners	0.624	0.526	0.335	118
Denver, 1982[c]				
Hispanic renters	0.045	0.097	0.032	62
Hispanic city areas	0.500*	0.400	0.100	16
Black renters	0.653*	0.369*	0.267*	70
Hispanic owners	0.427*	0.075	0.351*	72
Black owners	0.000	0.100	0.200	49
Anglo suburban areas	0.800*	0.400	0.000	21
Boston, 1983[d]				
Black renters	0.570	0.570	0.380	21
Hispanic renters	0.920	1.170	0.250	12
Southeast Asian renters	1.610	0.780	0.670	18
Black owners	0.302	0.430	0.358	38
Hispanic owners	0.446	0.599	0.205	25

[a]*Possibilities* = number of housing units discussed as serious possibilities; *Invited to see* = number of housing units invited to inspect; *Inspected* = number of housing units actually inspected.
[b]All entries significant at the 1 percent level.
[c]Overall figures include audits in minority city neighborhoods, Anglo city neighborhoods, and Anglo suburban neighborhoods. Entries marked with an asterisk are listed as statistically significant at the 5 percent level, but test used may understate statistical significance because a paired difference-of-means test was not used.
[d]Most entries significant at the 1 percent level; two significant at the 10 percent level only. Two audits for black renters not included because they are in a different neighborhood.
Sources: Boston 1981 data: Feins, Bratt, and Hollister, 1981. Denver data: James, McCummings, and Tynan, 1983. Boston 1983 data: Holshouser, 1984.

net measures exceed 25 percent, and many of the gross measures are close to 50 percent. These results are quite striking; as a lower bound estimate, minorities encounter discrimination in about one-quarter of their visits to housing agents; as an upper bound estimate, minorities encounter some discriminatory treatment in about half of their visits.

In most studies, all methods of measuring the probability of discrimination (the columns) yield similar results, although the probabilities tend to be somewhat smaller for discrimination concerning the advertised unit or actual inspections than for the other methods. In Wienk, Reid, Simonson, and Eggers (1979), the original index, in which an auditor is said to encounter discrimination if he or she is disfavored on at least one item and favored on none, and the alternative index, in which an auditor is said to encounter discrimination if he or she is disfavored more often than his or her teammate, yield similar probabilities. In Feins, Bratt, and Hollister (1981) and Holshouser (1984), however, the alternative index yields substantially higher probabilities than the original index. Overall, the probability of discrimination is high by most measures in most places.

The estimates in Table 3 apply to a single visit to a housing agent and therefore greatly understate the probability that a minority housing seeker who visits several agents will encounter some discrimination. Wienk, Reid, Simonson, and Eggers (1979) point out that with a constant (and independent) probability per visit, the probability of encountering at least one act of discrimination in N visits—say, $P(N)$—is given by the binomial density $P(N) = 1 - [1 - P(1)]^N$. Thus, a probability of discrimination on a single visit equal to 15 percent (below any of the gross measures in Table 3) implies that the probability of encountering at least one act of discrimination in 5 visits is 56 percent. A probability on a single visit of 50 percent implies that the probability in 5 visits is 97 percent. These results indicate that every black or Hispanic person who visits five or more housing agents in search of housing is far more likely than not to encounter some discrimination.

Lesson 3. Blacks, Hispanics, and perhaps Asian Americans all experience discrimination. Most of the audit studies focus on the treatment of blacks. As shown in Table 3, the level and probability of discrimination against blacks is high in most cases. Studies in Dallas, Denver, and Boston also examine discrimination against Hispanics. In all these cities (but not in all neighborhoods), Hispanics encounter discrimination. "Hispanic" is an ethnic distinction, not a racial one, and Hispanic Americans have a variety of different racial backgrounds, including Caucasian, American Indian, and black (see Simpson and Yinger, 1985). The Hakken study of Dallas indicates that only dark-skinned Hispanics—that is, Hispanics with black (and perhaps American Indian) ancestry—encounter statistically significant discrimination.

Only one study, Holshouser (1984), measures discrimination against Asian Americans. This study finds a high level of discrimination against Asian renters; indeed, on most measures Asians encounter more discrimination than either blacks or Hispanics. Because these results were based on the treatment of a single Asian auditor (in several audits), they need to be corroborated by other studies.

Lesson 4. Discrimination is concentrated in the flow of information about available housing, although it takes a variety of other forms in some cases. The existing evidence indicates that most discrimination involves a withholding of information about available housing. This finding should not blind us to the complexity of discriminatory behavior. Audit studies shed some light on this complexity by revealing patterns of discriminatory behavior across types of treatment and across neighborhoods.

Table 3. Estimated Probability of Discrimination in Housing Availability (in percents)

Sample	Advertised Unit	Possibilities	Invited to See	Inspected	Original Index	Alternate Index
40 SMSAs, 1977[b]						
Black renters						
Net	19	24	—	6	27	28
Gross	30	42	—	27	48	49
Black owners						
Net	10	30	15	10	15	18
Gross	21	54	46	38	39	47
Dallas, 1978[c]						
Dark-skinned Hispanic renters						
Net	—	37	29	—	43	—
Gross	—	47	36	—	55	—
Light-skinned Hispanic renters						
Net	—	15	11	—	16	—
Gross	—	32	24	—	39	—
Boston, 1981[d]						
Black renters						
Net	27	33	38	29	29	43
Gross	37	51	55	46	39	64
Black owners						
Net	15	30	24	25	24	37
Gross	21	46	43	38	43	61
Boston, 1981[e]						
Minority renters						
Net	18	48	39	33	53	71
Gross	23	56	49	38	59	77

Minority owners					
Net	−6	30	33	22	10	21
Gross	13	44	40	24	38	51

[a]*Advertised unit* = whether type of unit requested (national and Dallas studies) or advertised unit (Boston studies) was available; *possibilities* = number of housing units discussed as serious possibilities; *invited to see* = number of housing units invited to inspect; *inspected* = number of housing units actually inspected; *original index* = majority favored on at least one item; minority on none; *alternate index* = majority favored on more items than minority.

[b]All net measures significant at 1 percent level.

[c]Net measures significant at 1 percent level for dark-skinned Hispanics, not significant for light-skinned Hispanics.

[d]All net measures significant at 1 percent level.

[e]"Minority" includes blacks, Hispanics, and (for renters) Southeast Asians. All net measures significant at 1 percent level, except the two smallest positive entries for owners (5 percent level) and the one negative entry (not significant).

Sources: Data for 40 SMSAs: Wienk, Reid, Simonson, and Eggers, 1979. Data for Dallas: Hakken, 1979. Data for Boston in 1981: Feins, Bratt, and Hollister, 1981. Data for Boston in 1983: Holshouser, 1984.

Discrimination takes different forms in different places, and can be an effective barrier to housing access even when it does not involve information about available housing. Some agents, for example, advertise a housing unit that they are willing to show to minorities but reserve other available units for whites. This pattern of behavior does not appear to be common; discrimination in the number of serious possibilities offered tends to be accompanied by discrimination in showing the advertised unit. Nevertheless, it describes the treatment of blacks in Denver. Blacks in the Anglo suburbs are shown the advertised housing unit as often as whites but are told about similar houses only 33 percent of the time, compared with 40 percent for their teammates. Moreover, black renters in black neighborhoods of Denver are told the advertised unit is available more often than their white teammates (87 percent of the time versus 73 percent) but are told about similar units far less often (13 versus 40 percent).

The complexity of discrimination also appears in results concerning the provision of mortgage information. Wienk, Reid, Simonson, and Eggers (1979), Feins, Bratt, and Hollister (1981), and Holshouser (1984) all found that blacks faced significant discrimination in information about financing. In the national sample of Wienk, Reid, Simonson, and Eggers, the probability that the agent offered to help the auditor obtain financing was 47 percent for whites but only 38 percent for blacks. In Boston, in both 1981 and 1983, whites received far more suggestions about conventional and other financing than did blacks. James, McCummings, and Tynan (1983) discovered a different pattern of discrimination facing blacks in Denver. Within the City of Denver, blacks faced no discrimination in housing availability, but severe discrimination in information about financing. In Anglo city neighborhoods, for example, no black auditors, compared to 39 percent of the Anglo auditors, were offered suggestions about creative financing. This pattern was reversed in the suburbs; minorities encountered high levels of discrimination in housing availability but none in financing suggestions. Apparently, discrimination in Denver takes a different form in the city and in the suburbs.

Two studies, Pearce (1979) and Newberger (1984), provide information about steering, which is behavior designed to direct minorities toward certain locations. The Pearce study, which collected detailed geographic information on all the houses inspected by the auditors, involves 97 audits of real estate brokers in the Detroit area in 1974 and 1975. The audits in the Pearce (1979) study involve a gap of several weeks between teammates' visits. This feature complicates the interpretation of the study's findings on housing availability but has little effect on an interpretation of its results on steering. Pearce found that real estate brokers show blacks houses that are far removed from the brokers' business base. In fact, in the all-white southern, western, and eastern suburbs of Detroit, none of the houses shown to blacks, compared to 60 percent of the houses shown to whites, was in the community in which the real estate broker's office was located. Furthermore, virtually all the houses shown to blacks were either in and around the largely black western suburb of Inkster or in and around largely black areas of Detroit and its northern neighbors.

The Newberger study is based on the national audits conducted by Wienk, Reid, Simonson, and Eggers (1979). Newberger determined whether blacks were shown houses in census tracts with a higher percentage of blacks than the tracts in which whites were shown houses. The percentage of blacks was higher for the black auditor in 517 audits and for the white auditor in 299 audits. This difference, which is highly significant statistically, indicates that blacks were steered into largely black tracts.

Lesson 5. The main cause of discrimination in housing is economic—that is, housing agents cater to the prejudice of their white customers—although some evidence indicates that agent prejudice is also at work. Fair housing audits not only provide a direct measure of discrimination but also allow researchers to test hypotheses about the causes of discriminatory behavior by housing agents. Any such hypothesis is a statement about the circumstances that induce agents to discriminate. By collecting information on the circumstances surrounding an audit, a researcher can determine whether the circumstances identified by a hypothesis in fact lead to discrimination.

The literature contains two principal hypotheses about the causes of racial discrimination by housing agents. For a more detailed discussion of these hypotheses, see Simonson and Wienk (1984) and Yinger (1986). The customer prejudice hypothesis states that an agent who relies on the business of prejudiced whites discriminates in order to avoid alienating current or potential white customers. Rental agents want to avoid the costs associated with rapid turnover. The rental agent for an all-white apartment building may therefore discriminate against blacks because renting to even a few blacks could lead to the exit of many or all white tenants. Real estate brokers attempt to attract potential buyers and sellers by building a reputation and cultivating contacts in their community. In a prejudiced white community, brokers who sell to blacks will have a bad reputation, so brokers in such communities discriminate against blacks to avoid alienating their potential white clients. Furthermore, housing agents are more likely to discriminate against the blacks who are most likely to upset their white customers, namely lower-income blacks or blacks with school-age chidren.

Racial transition weakens these incentives to discriminate. Suppose blacks are willing to pay more than whites for apartments in a particular largely white neighborhood. Landlords in that neighborhood may be willing to rent to blacks because racial transition increases rental income enough to compensate for the turnover costs. In the sales market, a real estate broker cannot be blamed for introducing blacks if racial transition has already started; in this case, he or she may be able to generate extra commission income by encouraging rapid housing turnover.

The agent prejudice hypothesis is that housing agents themselves are prejudiced against blacks and discriminate to avoid dealing with them. This hypothesis predicts that those housing agents most likely to be prejudiced are the most likely to discriminate. Several studies have found that older people are more prejudiced than younger people and that men are more prejudiced than women (see Schuman, Steed, and Bobo, 1985). According to this hypothesis, therefore, older agents will discriminate more than younger agents, and male agents will discriminate more than female agents. This hypothesis also predicts that some types of minority auditors may encounter more discrimination than others. In particular, agents may be more prejudiced against black men than against black women and may therefore discriminate more heavily against black men.

Simonson and Wienk (1984) examine the causes of discrimination in the audits collected by Wienk, Reid, Simonson, and Eggers (1979) in forty metropolitan areas in 1977. They employ regression analysis to determine the impact on the probability of discrimination of the characteristics of the agent, the auditor, and neighborhood, and the metropolitan area. Their dependent variables are the probability measures in Columns 1 and 4 of Table 3. They find that both customer and agent prejudice are causes of discrimination by housing agents. As predicted by the customer-prejudice hypothesis, for example, discrimination is lower against higher-income blacks. And, as predicted by the agent-prejudice hypothesis, discrimination is higher by older agents and by male agents.

Yinger (1986) uses a similar regression methodology to test these two hypotheses using the 1981 Boston audit data collected by Feins, Bratt, and Hollister (1981). Three dependent variables are examined, namely the levels of discrimination in housing availability as reported in Table 2. Yinger finds that discrimination in showing houses for sale is stronger against the black households that would most upset white customers, namely low-income blacks and black families with children. Moreover, Yinger finds that discrimination is high in all-white areas and low or nonexistent in areas undergoing rapid racial transition. These results indicate that customer prejudice is the primary cause of discrimination.

Yinger also uncovers evidence that agents' own prejudice sometimes can lead to discrimination. In the sales audits in Boston, married black women encounter less discrimination in actual inspections than do married black men. Both brokers and their white customers might be more prejudiced against black men than against black women. When a black couple moves in, however, white residents have both spouses as neighbors, whereas the broker must deal only with the spouse who does the housing search. This finding therefore must reflect broker prejudice—not white customer prejudice. Overall, Yinger's results suggest that agent prejudice is a relatively minor cause of discrimination.

Thus, the primary cause of discrimination in housing appears to be economic; housing agents in largely white areas discriminate against blacks because they believe it is in their economic interest to cater to the prejudice of their white customers. In addition, some housing agents appear to discriminate because of their own racial prejudice.

Conclusion

Fair housing audits are a powerful new technique for studying racial and ethnic discrimination. Five high-quality audit studies all find high levels of discrimination against minorities in the provision of information about available housing and/or high probabilities that minorities will encounter such discrimination. These studies cover many cities over the years 1977–1983, so one can safely conclude that widespread discrimination persists in the United States today despite existing civil rights legislation.

Audit studies also reveal that discrimination hits blacks, Hispanics, and Asian Americans, that discrimination is a complex phenomenon that takes different forms in different circumstances, and that the primary cause of discrimination appears to be the desire of housing agents to please their prejudiced white customers.

The rigorous audit methodology makes this evidence very compelling. Audits measure discrimination directly and therefore, unlike previous research on discrimination, do not rely on abstract theories of household residential location or on elaborate econometric techniques. Thus, existing audit evidence builds a strong case for stricter, more effective antidiscrimination legislation. This legislation also could be improved by recognizing one of the lessons from audit studies, namely that the primary cause of discrimination appears to be economic. As Yinger (1987) and others have pointed out, antidiscrimination legislation is unlikely to be effective unless it offsets the economic incentives that induce housing agents to discriminate.

References

Feins, J. D., and Bratt, R. G. "Barred in Boston: Racial Discrimination in Housing." *APA Journal,* Summer, 1983, pp. 344–355.
Feins, J. D., Bratt, R. G., and Hollister, R. *Final Report of a Study of Racial Discrimination in the Boston Housing Market.* Cambridge, Mass.: Abt Associates, 1981.

Hakken, J. *Discrimination Against Chicanos in the Dallas Rental Housing Market: An Experimental Extension of the Housing Market Practices Survey.* Washington, D.C.: U.S. Department of Housing and Urban Development, 1979.

Holshouser, W. *Final Report of a Study of Racial Discrimination in Two Boston Housing Markets.* Cambridge, Mass.: Abt Associates, 1984.

James, F. J., McCummings, B. L., and Tynan, E. A. *Discrimination, Segregation, and Minority Housing Conditions in Sunbelt Cities: A Study of Denver, Houston, and Phoenix.* Denver: Center for Public-Private Sector Cooperation, Graduate School of Public Affairs, University of Colorado at Denver, 1983.

McIntosh, N., and Smith, D. J. *The Extent of Racial Discrimination.* London: PEP, 1974.

Newberger, H. "The Nature and Extent of Racial Steering Practices in the U.S. Housing Market." Unpublished manuscript, U.S. Department of Housing and Urban Development, Washington, D.C., 1981.

Newberger, H. *Recent Evidence on Discrimination in Housing.* Washington, D.C.: U.S. Department of Housing and Urban Development, 1984.

Pearce, D. M. "Gatekeepers and Homeseekers: Institutional Patterns in Racial Steering." *Social Problems,* 1979, 3, 325-342.

Schafer, R., and Ladd, H. F. *Discrimination in Mortgage Lending.* Cambridge, Mass.: MIT Press, 1981.

Schuman, H., Steed, C., and Bobo, L. *Racial Attitudes in America.* Cambridge, Mass.: Harvard University Press, 1985.

Simonson, J. C., and Wienk, R. E. "Racial Discrimination in Housing Sales: An Empirical Test of Alternative Models of Broker Behavior." Unpublished manuscript, Office of the U.S. Comptroller of Currency, Washington, D.C., 1984.

Simpson, G. E., and Yinger, J. M. *Racial and Cultural Minorities: An Analysis of Prejudice and Discrimination.* 5th ed. New York: Plenum Press, 1985.

Wienk, R. E., Reid, C. E., Simonson, J. C., and Eggers, F. C. *Measuring Discrimination in American Housing Markets: The Housing Market Practices Survey.* Washington, D.C.: U.S. Department of Housing and Urban Development, 1979.

Yinger, J. "Prejudice and Discrimination in the Urban Housing Market." In P. Mieszkowski and M. Straszheim (eds.), *Current Issues in Urban Economics.* Johns Hopkins University Press, 1979.

Yinger, J. "Measuring Racial and Ethnic Discrimination with Fair Housing Audits: A Review of Existing Evidence and Research Methodology." Paper submitted to the HUD Conference on Fair Housing Testing, December 6-7, 1984, Washington, D.C.

Yinger, J. "Measuring Racial Discrimination with Fair Housing Audits: Caught in the Act." *American Economic Review,* Dec. 1986, pp. 881-893.

Yinger, J. "The Racial Dimension of Urban Housing Markets in the 1980s." In G. Tobin (ed.), *Divided Neighborhoods: Changing Patterns of Racial Segregation in the 1980s.* Newbury Park, Calif.: Sage, 1987.

John Yinger is professor of economics and public administration at the Maxwell School, Syracuse University. He has published extensively on issues of housing economics, discrimination, and urban public finance.

Over the past several decades, skepticism about the effectiveness of juvenile delinquency interventions has increased substantially. However, as the quality of research on this topic has improved, a more optimistic perspective has begun to emerge. To address this issue, the author summarizes three meta-analyses indicating that interventions to reduce juvenile delinquency may have small but meaningful positive impacts. This systematic literature review also suggests promising avenues for future research.

Juvenile Delinquency Intervention

Mark W. Lipsey

One can argue that the crime problem in society is in a very direct way a juvenile delinquency problem. Criminal activity shows strong age relations, increasing sharply from about age ten to age eighteen, then decreasing thereafter (Elliott and Huizinga, 1984, pp. 60–67) with the result that about 40 percent of all arrests for FBI index crimes are juveniles (Flanagan, van Alstyne, and Gottfredson, 1982). Moreover, most people who become chronic offenders begin during adolescence or before (Loeber, 1982).

These circumstances highlight the importance of interventions that target juvenile delinquency and attempt to suppress or prevent it in various ways. The potential payoff of such programs is twofold. First, if they are successful in lowering the incidence of juvenile offenses, crime generally is decreased since such large proportions stem from juveniles. Secondly, if they are successful in disrupting patterns of chronic offense at an early juvenile stage, they may head off a large proportion of the adult criminality that ensues as chronic juvenile offenders become chronic adult offenders.

In addition to the strong practical reasons for desiring effective intervention for juvenile crime, important humane values are at stake as well. Our society recognizes adolescence as a period of transition to adulthood where experimentation takes place, judgment is immature, and a guiding hand is often required to point a youth in socially constructive directions. Our juvenile courts are historically based in the concept of *parens patriae*, embodying the notion that juvenile offenders should be treated differently from adults—more forgivingly and with more attention to the effects on their subsequent development.

For these various reasons, it is especially interesting to ask, "What have we learned from evaluation of juvenile delinquency intervention?"

The Background

We will pick up the story around the mid 1970s, where two different but complementary developments were taking place, one in the political arena and one in the research arena. During this period, the rehabilitative ethic in criminal justice began to come under effective attack. The primary focus was the prison system, largely constructed on the premise that, with isolation from harmful influences and a regimen of discipline and self-development, prisoners could be rehabilitated and returned to society as useful citizens. The clearest manifestation of this ethic was the indeterminate sentence, the notion that a prisoner would not serve fixed time but would be held until "ready" for release. The reality of high recidivism rates among prisoners and the rise of political conservatism, with a more punitive attitude toward criminals, brought this model under attack. Moreover, liberal defenders of the model were themselves becoming disenchanted with it, recognizing that the indeterminate sentence often served only to prolong the stay of offenders in relatively harsh, inhumane prison conditions (Cullen and Gilbert, 1982).

The new paradigm for the criminal justice system increasingly has come to be the "justice model" or, as it is sometimes called, the "just desserts" model. In this view, the role of the criminal justice system is to apprehend and sanction offenders, not to rehabilitate them. We see the implementation of this model in the rush of state legislatures to adopt stiff mandatory penalties for an increasingly wide range of offenses, the return of determinate sentences, and sharply decreased political support for rehabilitation programs.

These developments were in no way impeded by the extensive evaluation research that had been done over the years on the effectiveness of various offender treatment and rehabilitation programs. On the contrary, in a remarkable, but not necessarily independent, confluence of trends this era was marked by a series of dramatic, well-publicized research reviews concluding that rehabilitative treatment was ineffective.

Most notorious among the reviews of the evaluation literature was Lipton, Martinson, and Wilks's (1975) broad survey of research on correctional treatments. In a massive volume (735 pages), they made a detailed examination of 231 separate studies involving interventions at all phases of the law enforcement and criminal justice system for both juveniles and adults. Martinson's (1974, p. 25) widely quoted conclusion was that "with few and isolated exceptions, the rehabilitative efforts that have been reported so far have had no appreciable effect on recidivism." Greenberg (1977), who updated the Lipton, Martinson, and Wilks review, echoed that pessimism: "The blanket assertion that 'nothing works' is an exaggeration, but not by very much" (p. 141).

These broad reviews tarred delinquency treatment programs with the same brush that covered other rehabilitative efforts for criminal offenders. Reviews that focused directly on delinquency treatment efforts, however, reached similar conclusions. Romig (1978), for example, made an optimistic attempt to identify the characteristics of successful treatment of delinquents, cataloguing the available studies with a level of detail rivaling that of Lipton, Martinson, and Wilks. In each category of treatment, he found relatively few positive results to report. A more critical stance on the delinquency prevention research literature was taken by Wright and Dixon (1977) and by Lundman, McFarlane, and Scarpitti (1976). They, too, reached essentially negative conclusions about the effectiveness of prevention programs, finding little evidence of significant preventive effects on juvenile crime.

The Foreground

It may seem from this brief history that what we have learned is that treatment programs for juvenile delinquency do not work and are not politically popular—a conclusion quite compatible with the current political climate, government budget stringencies, and pessimism about large-scale social programs (for example, see Murray, 1985; Rossi and Wright, 1984). The story does not end here, however. Indeed, it appears that a new chapter is just beginning. In recent years, significant challenges have been raised both to the political perspective on offender rehabilitation and to the research perspective.

The more optimistic view of treatment that is emerging seems to have resulted from two factors. First, it is increasingly being recognized that the attempt to provide treatment and rehabilitation has a humanizing effect on criminal justice institutions, especially prisons, entirely separate from any direct effects those treatments might have on the offenders (Cullen and Gilbert, 1982). Secondly, there have been important new research developments. On the one hand, some promising areas for treatment have been identified and explored sufficiently to establish the potential for results. On the other hand, retrospective criticism has considerably sharpened researchers' understanding of what is required to evaluate a treatment program in criminal justice. It is these developments in evaluation research to which I now turn—they constitute the most important aspects of what has been learned about juvenile delinquency interventions in recent years.

The New Evaluation Research

The important recent research developments in juvenile delinquency treatment are framed by the two reports of the National Academy of Sciences (NAS) Panel on Research on Rehabilitative Techniques (Sechrest, White, and Brown, 1979; Martin, Sechrest, and Redner, 1981). The first report carefully combed through the available treatment evaluation research and reviews of that research, then reluctantly concluded that there was indeed little evidence of successful treatment for either juveniles or adults: "Although a generous reviewer of the literature might discern some glimmers of hope, those glimmers are so few, so scattered, and so inconsistent that they do not serve as a basis for any recommendation other than continued research" (Sechrest, White, and Brown, 1979, p. 3). *But* they emphasized the possibility that the problem was the nature of the evidence rather than failure of the concept. "The one positive conclusion is discouraging: the research methodology that has been brought to bear on the problem of finding ways to rehabilitate criminal offenders has been generally so inadequate that only a relatively few studies warrant any unequivocal interpretations" (Sechrest, White, and Brown, 1979, p. 3).

In particular, they identified a variety of factors essential to credible evaluation research on this topic and ruefully noted that virtually no studies measured up to what was required. Their conclusion, therefore, was that no conclusion about the efficacy of offender treatment could be drawn until much better research was done. This point, coupled with many other similar observations (for example, Berleman, 1980; Lundman and Scarpitti, 1978; Quay, 1977), has gradually affected evaluation practice so that we now have at least a clear appreciation of what is required even if individual efforts only approximate that ideal.

The second NAS report was itself a remarkable development. Given the uncertainty of the evidence studied in the first report, the committee felt compelled to continue its work in order to identify promising treatment developments for which the pessimistic generalizations from other research might not apply. Their attention turned to various key "loci of intervention"—the individual, the family, the school, the workplace, and the community (including peer group)—only one of which (the individual) had received much examination in the research literature.

In some sense, all subsequent significant developments in juvenile delinquency intervention research have been footnotes to one of these two reports (although the authors of such work have not necessarily viewed it that way). These two reports, published as recently as 1979 and 1981 respectively, provide their own elegant and comprehensive answer to the question "What have we learned about juvenile delinquency intervention?" The task that remains now is to update those statements with a report of subsequent developments.

Two important developments over the last five years command attention. First, we have mounting evidence of the efficacy of delinquency treatment on a broad front, in contrast to the discouragingly null results of the research available prior to 1980. This more general evidence of the possibility of treatment efficacy is buttressed by some specific programs of intervention and research that have continued to mature since 1980, with increasingly positive yield. Second, we have continued to refine our understanding of what is needed in the way of treatment rationale and regimen and research methods to do credible "state of the art" research on delinquency intervention.

The Possibility of Treatment Efficacy. For purposes of making a broad assessment of treatment effects, the most important development since the NAS reports has been the rise of meta-analysis, a technique for statistically aggregating the results of a body of research and analyzing them as a single data set (Glass, McGaw, and Smith, 1981; Hedges and Olkin, 1985; Hunter, Schmidt, and Jackson, 1982; Rosenthal, 1984). Largely because of the increased statistical power that comes through such aggregation, meta-analysis of treatment evaluation research often reveals positive overall effects even when the individual studies going into the meta-analysis are heavy with null results. For example, the classic Smith and Glass (1977; see also Smith, Glass, and Miller, 1980) meta-analysis of psychotherapy effectiveness research showed relatively substantial and widespread positive effects despite a long history of ambiguity and controversy among reviewers.

What we need at this point is a comprehensive meta-analysis of delinquency treatment with results that can be interpreted directly and compared with those in related treatment areas. Such an effort is underway (by Mark W. Lipsey under National Institute of Mental Health (NIMH) funding; grant no. MH 39958, "Meta-Analysis of Juvenile Delinquency Treatment Research," awarded through the Antisocial and Violent Behavior Branch, National Institute of Mental Health; and funding from the Russell Sage Foundation), but results are not yet available. Three smaller-scale meta-analyses have been conducted, however, on different subsets of available delinquency treatment research, and all have yielded somewhat encouraging results.

Tables 1, 2, and 3 summarize the results of these three delinquency meta-analyses. The most extensive of the three was conducted by Garrett (1984, 1985) who focused on adjudicated delinquents placed in residential facilities, either community or institutional. She examined the effects of

Table 1. Summary of Garrett Delinquency Treatment Meta-Analysis

Inclusion Criteria: Residential treatment, adjudicated delinquents, published and unpublished research since 1960.

Sample: 111 studies, 225 comparisons, 433 effect sizes (Glass d).

Item 1. Overall mean effect sizes (ES): stronger designs versus weaker designs[a]

0.24 = mean ES, random/matched/pretest-equated designs ("more rigorous")
  (0.23 for random versus 0.41 for matched, pretest-equated, convenience)
0.65 = mean ES, pre-, post-, and other nonrandom designs ("less rigorous")

Item 2. Treatment × outcome ES for "more rigorous" studies (N = 58)

Outcome Measure	Psychodynamic[b]	Behavioral[c]	Life Skills[d]	Other[e]	Raw	Weighted
Recidivism	-0.01(10)	-0.08 (6)	0.30 (3)	0.33 (5)	0.10	0.14(19)
Institutional adjustment	0.30(14)	0.33(14)	-0.08 (2)	0.11 (5)	0.27	0.17(29)
Psychological adjustment	0.48(19)	0.58(13)	1.31 (1)	0.33(10)	0.45	0.68(34)
Community adjustment	0.91 (4)	—	0.38 (2)	1.02 (3)	0.72	0.78 (7)
Academic	0.34 (2)	0.61 (5)	0.42 (2)	0.01 (2)	0.42	0.35 (8)
Vocational adjustment	0.58 (1)	-0.23 (1)	-0.04 (1)	0.06 (2)	0.06	0.09 (4)
Other	0.64 (3)	0.17 (2)	0.42 (2)	—	0.44	0.41 (6)
All Measures						
Raw means	0.17(27)	0.30(22)	0.32 (5)	0.27(11)	0.24(58)	
Equal weighted	0.46	0.23	0.39	0.31		

Item 3. Other breakdowns by ES for "more rigorous" studies (N = 58)

Male	0.22(47)	Setting		Duration	
Female	0.54 (9)	Institution	0.25(52)	0–12 weeks	0.56(25)
		Community	-0.01 (6)	>12 weeks	0.09(28)
Age	<15 0.34(12)	Contact Frequency			
	15–17 0.27(33)	Daily	0.22(23)		
	>17 0.12(19)	2–4/week	0.25(19)		
		1/week	0.27(12)		

Note: In all cases, numbers in parentheses are N of studies.
[a] No statistical significance tests reported for overall mean effect sizes.
[b] Psychodynamic = individual, group, family counseling.
[c] Behavioral = contingency management, cognitive-behavioral, guided group interaction, positive peer culture, milieu.
[d] Life skills = drug-alcohol, academic, vocational, outdoor.
[e] Other = music therapy, megavitamins, small unit size, unspecified "skills."
Source: Garrett, 1984, 1985.

treatment programs in such facilities on a wide range of outcome variables. On the other end of the spectrum, Kaufman (1985) restricted his meta-analysis to "prevention" treatment of preadjudicated at-risk juveniles, looking only at delinquency outcome measures used in randomized research designs. The meta-analysis by Davidson, Gottschalk, Gensheimer, and Mayer (1984) fell somewhere between these other two efforts. It included only treatment of adjudicated delinquents but was not restricted to treatment in residential facilities; indeed, only about half the sample was residential.

This is not the place for a detailed examination of the results of these three meta-analyses, and each study has shortcomings for present purposes. The overall pattern of their results, however, is instructive and relatively encouraging. All three meta-analyses found that the grand mean effect size for the better-designed studies, averaged over all studies and outcome measures, was positive—ranging from around one-fourth to one-third of a standard deviation of treatment group superiority over control group outcome.

We may be encouraged by the positive direction of effects shown in these meta-analyses; however, we might still be skeptical of the order of magnitude. Is one-fourth to one-third of a standard deviation an effect of practical significance? In familiar variance terms, these figures represent 1.5 and 2.7 percent of the variance, respectively—seemingly unimpressive. Recent scrutiny of effect size indices, however, has revealed that small orders of magnitude in percent variance (or standard deviation) terms can correspond to large effects in practical terms (Abelson, 1985; Rosenthal and Rubin, 1982). A translation of these figures into dichotomous success rates, for example, reveals that an effect of 0.25 standard deviation is equivalent to the difference between a 44 percent success rate in the control group versus a 56 percent success rate in the treatment group; 0.33 standard deviation, correspondingly, represents a contrast between 42 percent control group success versus 58 percent treatment group success (Rosenthal and Rubin, 1982). A treatment that increases the success rate by 12 to 16 percentage points might well be judged practically significant. By way of comparison, Lipsey (1982, 1983) has shown that the difference on arrest measures between those juveniles the police "counsel and release" to the custody of their parents (relatively minor offenders) and those they send to the juvenile courts (more serious offenders) amounts to 3 percent of the variance; that is, about one-third of a standard deviation difference. Thus, the practical distinctions police officers make regarding the severity of arrested juveniles are on about the same order of magnitude as the treatment effects demonstrated by the meta-analyses. The piecemeal results currently available from delinquency treatment meta-analyses, therefore, seem to indicate treatment effects that are positive and potentially nontrivial.

Table 2. Summary of Kaufman Delinquency Treatment Meta-Analysis

Inclusion Criteria: Preadjudicated "prevention" delinquents, studies with randomized control designs and delinquency outcome measures, published and unpublished research.

Sample: 20 studies, 53 effect sizes (Glass d).

Item 1. Overall mean effect sizes (ES)[a]

0.20 = mean ES, delinquency measures only
0.25 = mean ES, delinquency measures first averaged within study

Item 2. Mean effect size for different treatments (delinquency measures only)[b]

Treatment	Mean ES	Significance Level
Counseling	-0.00 (4)	ns
Services	0.08 (7)	ns
Contingency cont.	0.36 (3)	0.01
Casework	0.29 (3)	ns
Job Training	0.50 (4)	ns

Item 3. Mean effect size for different delinquency measures[c]

Measure	Mean ES	Significance Level
Police referrals/contacts	0.24 (11)	ns
Petitions to court	0.10 (7)	ns
Recorded arrests	-0.02 (2)	ns
Self-report	0.98 (1)	0.1

Item 4. Mean effect size for different amounts of contact time[d]

Contact Frequency	Mean ES
Low (0.1-2 hrs/wk)	0.15 (8)
High (2.1-16 hrs/wk)	0.63 (7)

[a] Mean effect sizes reported as statistically significant.
[b] N of studies in parentheses. Significance based on multiple regression with treatment frequency and duration, type of recidivism measure partialed out.
[c] N of studies in parentheses. Significance based on multiple regression with treatment frequency and duration partialed out.
[d] Missing data on five studies prohibits inclusion in regression analysis.

Source: Kaufman, 1985.

In addition to assessing the order of magnitude of overall treatment effects, meta-analysis also often permits examination of the relationships between effect size and such factors as treatment modality, client characteristics, and research design. Although these three delinquency treatment meta-analyses are too limited to support any strong conclusions about such relations, the pattern of results on such matters is worth at least a brief summary, if for no other reason than to illustrate the difficulty of interpreting meta-analysis results:

Table 3. Summary of Davidson and others Delinquency Treatment Meta-Analysis

Inclusion Criteria: Police- and court-referred delinquents, published studies, 1967-1983.

Sample: 91 studies, N of effect sizes not reported, Glass d used.

Item 1. Overall mean effect sizes (ES): stronger designs versus weaker designs[a]

0.35 = mean ES for experimental and comparison group (EC) designs ($N = 68$)
    (Correlation of ES with random versus nonrandom assignment = 0.15)
0.75 = mean ES for pre-/post-/(PP) designs ($N = 28$)

Item 2. Mean effect size for different outcome measures (EC studies only)[b]

Measure	Mean ES	Significance Level
Recidivism	0.32(58)	ns
Self-reported delinquency	0.14 (3)	ns
Behavioral outcomes	0.49(22)	ns
Attitude outcomes	0.38(16)	ns

Item 3. Correlations between ES and treatment type (includes pre-/post-/studies)

Negative		Not Significant	Positive	
Group therapy	$r = -0.18$	Modeling	Academic	$r = 0.25$
Transactional	$r = -0.17$	Token economy	Positive	
		Behavioral contract	reinforcement	$r = 0.19$
		Probation	Service broker	$r = 0.20$
		Casework	Vocational	$r = 0.22$
		Advocacy		
		Psychodynamic		
		Client centered		
		Cognitive therapy		
		Reality therapy		

Item 4. Correlations between ES and client, treatment characteristics

No correlations with age, sex, setting (community, residential)
No correlations with total number of treatment hours, duration of treatment

[a] Mean ES statistically nonsignificant for EC designs; significant for PP designs.
[b] N of studies in parentheses. Significance based on confidence limits.
Source: Davidson, Gottschalk, Gensheimer, and Mayer, 1984.

Treatment Modality. No consistent picture emerges here. Garrett (1985) found psychodynamic treatment best, life skills training (academic and vocational) nearly as good, and behavioral approaches weakest. Kaufman (1985) and Davidson, Gottschalk, Gensheimer, and Mayer (1984) found behavioral approaches (at least some categories) stronger than psychodynamic approaches. Davidson, Gottschalk, Gensheimer, and Mayer concurred with Garrett on the relative efficacy of life skills training, however. What is most abundantly clear is how misleading it is to make simple comparisons among modalities on the basis of mean effect size. Analyses by Kaufman and Garrett show that modality is confounded with treatment intensity, variation and differences in outcome measures used, which, when partialed out, result in various rearrangements of the rank order of modalities on effect size.

Treatment Intensity, Frequency, Duration. No consistent picture emerged here either. Garrett found no relation between contact frequency and effect size; Davidson, Gottschalk, Gensheimer, and Mayer similarly found no relation between total number of hours of treatment or total duration of treatment. Kaufman, however, found that for his "prevention" studies, hours per week of contact (divided at the median) was strongly related to effect size.

Client Characteristics. None of the meta-analysts found sufficiently detailed reporting of client characteristics to support much analysis. Davidson, Gottschalk, Gensheimer, and Mayer (1984) found no correlation between (1) effect size and (2) age, sex, or treatment setting. Garrett, however, found a relationship with sex (larger effects for females) and setting (larger effects in institutions).

Outcome Measures. All three studies found large differences among various categories of outcome measures. Generally recidivism measures based on official police or court records showed the smallest effects, behavioral and "adjustment" measures showed the largest effects. Self-report delinquency was used in too few studies to support conclusions.

Research Design. Effect size showed a strong relationship to research design. In particular, before-and-after designs greatly overestimated effects relative to random assignment control designs (Garrett, 1985; Davidson, Gottschalk, Gensheimer, and Mayer, 1984). Results were inconsistent with regard to differences between random and nonrandom assignment to control groups. Garrett found smaller effects with random assignment; Davidson, Gottschalk, Gensheimer, and Mayer found larger effects.

Meta-analysis represents something of a "lowest common denominator" approach to assessing treatment efficacy. That is, it examines the average effects of the average study using the average treatment, measures, and research design. Alternatively, we can proceed by demonstrating that certain well-conceived, well-implemented, and well-researched treatments have positive effects. Indeed, positive meta-analysis results would not be credible if at least some of the exemplary cases of treatment and research did not also yield positive results.

Space limitations preclude a full review of the major exemplary research programs, but fortunately they are well documented elsewhere. Ross and Gendreau (1980; Gendreau and Ross, 1979) have identified many such studies that produce positive results. Especially notable are several major, sustained programs of research that have not only shown positive effects in controlled studies but also have provided a wealth of useful detail about delinquency, treatment, and research methods; for example, the work at the Oregon Social Learning Center based on social learning concepts (Patterson, 1985, 1986; Patterson, Chamberlain, and Reid, 1982), the Kansas teaching family model based on behavioral principles (Braukman, Kirigin, and Wolf, 1980; Kirigin, Braukman, Atwater, and Wolf, 1982; Wolf and others, 1976), and the exploration of diversion services provided by student volunteers (Davidson and others, 1977; Davidson and others, forthcoming).

Doing State-of-the-Art Evaluation Research on Delinquency Treatments. The most important aspect of demonstrating the possibility of delinquency treatment efficacy is that it opens the way for expanded exploration of new approaches to treatment rather than suffocating such efforts under the presumption that "nothing works." What is called for here is a joining of promising treatment concepts with a research paradigm that reflects hard-won trial-and-error knowledge of what is required to adequately develop, implement, document, and test those treatment concepts. Of the range of promising treatment approaches that can be generated from existing theory and clinical experience, only a very few have actually been subjected to anything approaching adequate research. Much of what has been learned in recent decades about delinquency treatment evaluation is how such research should be done. I turn now to a review of the key methodological concepts that collectively constitute a framework for conducting "state-of-the-art" research on delinquency treatment effectiveness. In undertaking such a review, I necessarily find myself restating and updating many of the points so cogently made by the NAS panel in its broader review of research on offender rehabilitation (Sechrest, White, and Brown, 1979).

In brief, we want to consider six concepts that are integral to an adequate research framework for delinquency treatment:

1. There must be a detailed and defensible treatment theory to guide the intervention and the selection of research variables.

2. The target juveniles to whom the treatment is to be applied must be specified carefully and their risk of subsequent delinquency established.

3. The treatment must be sufficiently strong to be plausible and be implemented with a high degree of integrity (or quality control); in addition, the extent of the implementation must be documented empirically.

4. Appropriate and sensitive dependent measures must be used, and they should be accompanied by measures of key intervening variables and covariates.

5. Treatment versus control comparisons should be configured to have high statistical power; that is, to be capable of statistically detecting treatment effects of the expected order of magnitude.

6. The research design should permit valid causal inference about treatment effects and be sensitive to interactions as well as main effects.

A brief expansion of each of these points follows.

Treatment Theory. Juvenile delinquency does not occur through a known, or even a single set of causes; nor does it have a single set of symptoms. These circumstances make it difficult to construct a rationale for treatment and encourage trial-and-error experimentation in which various hunches and pet programs are applied more or less systematically on a "Let's see if it works" basis. The accompanying research represents treatment as a "black box"—an undifferentiated package that one experimental group receives and another does not. Although a certain amount of trial-and-error testing of clinical hunches may well open up promising avenues, this approach has too many problems to justify its popularity.

First, it provides little basis for identifying the optimal points for intervention and no basis for determining what constitutes sufficient treatment—what regimen and what intensity or strength of treatment are best matched to the target problem. Secondly, this approach offers little explanatory power for either success or failure. If the treatment is effective, it is difficult to replicate or generalize without knowing the sources of its success so that the essential features can be distinguished from the superfluous ones. If it is ineffective, little basis exists for explaining why and identifying the means to improve it. Finally, the black box approach leaves the research process woefully open-ended—little basis exists for determining what variables are important to measure or what range of outcomes might reasonably be expected.

Since the NAS report, notable progress has been made toward better treatment theory. Two different examples serve to illustrate recent work. Patterson and his colleagues at the Oregon Social Learning Center have pursued this matter at two levels. First, they have embarked on a longitudinal inquiry into family processes and the factors that contribute to the development of delinquency, such as parental discipline and monitoring (Patterson, 1986). Secondly, they have begun to evolve treatment microtheories that deal with the interaction process between therapist and client, such as parental resistance (Patterson, 1985). Taking a different tack, Gottfredson (1984) has pioneered an approach that relies on the collaboration of researchers and treatment personnel to articulate treatment theory as a basis for strengthening both treatment programs and the evaluation research conducted on them.

Targeting Juveniles. A simple but important truism for delinquency treatment is that you cannot treat what is not there. Delinquency is not a condition, but a behavior; more precisely, a pattern of behavior. Treatment can only be effective on juveniles who can be expected to establish a pattern of delinquent behavior in the absence of treatment. An important fact of delinquency is that many (indeed most) adolescents act in a delinquent manner on occasion. Even when the behavior is sufficient to bring the incident to the attention of the police, however, it does not follow that the juvenile is delinquent in the sense of having a continuing pattern of delinquency. Birth cohort panel studies (Griffiths and Jesness, 1981; Wolfgang, Figlio, and Sellin, 1972) have shown that approximately 45 of every 100 juveniles arrested have no subsequent arrests. Even among those arrested twice, about one-third have no subsequent arrests. Thus attempting to identify delinquents on the basis of officially recorded incidents of delinquent behavior, which otherwise seems like a very straightforward approach, yields high proportions who have virtually no risk of subsequent delinquency, at least as indexed by police contacts.

The situation is further complicated by the findings from the National Youth Survey indicating that only a small proportion (14 percent) of chronic delinquents identified from self-report data were arrested even once (Dunford and Elliott, 1984; Elliott, Dunford, and Huizinga, 1986). Thus the overwhelming majority of chronic delinquents are not identifiable from police records and the large majority of those juveniles arrested are not chronic delinquents.

Despite the difficulties in selecting at-risk youth straightforwardly from official records, great strides have been made in recent years in identifying chronically antisocial youth in ways that permit them to be selected for intervention. Most important has been the linking of antisocial behavior to developmental sequences originating well before adolescence (Loeber, 1982). An increasingly wide range of predictors have been identified as having some ability to predict subsequent chronic delinquency (Loeber and Stouthamer-Loeber, 1986; in press).

As a practical matter, using a range of these predictor variables to select juveniles for treatment can be cumbersome and expensive. An attractive approach is sequential selection or "multiple gating" (Loeber, Dishion, and Patterson, 1984). In this procedure, a broad, inexpensive screening technique is used first (for example, teacher ratings). Those juveniles identified as potential problems in this screening then receive closer examination (such as a telephone interview with parents) on a second screening. Those still identified as potential problems might then receive a final assessment that may include face-to-face interviews and various diagnostic tests. (For other discussions of multiple gating, see Loeber and Stouthamer-Loeber, in press; Reid, Baldwin, Patterson, and Dishion, in press.)

Implementation. Another truism of delinquency treatment research is that treatment that is not delivered cannot be expected to have effects. More important in practice is the corollary that a weak treatment can be expected to have weak effects. Two inherent features make delinquency treatment difficult to deliver. First, the clients (juveniles and/or their families) often do not volunteer for treatment except under coercion and are thus resistant and often hostile to treatment. Secondly, delinquents are frequently not in stable life situations. They may not have reliable transportation, housing, friends, or family and may live amid considerable turmoil and disruption. Getting them to a treatment facility or tracking them down on a regular basis for treatment elsewhere may be very difficult. Even institutionalized juveniles may be unreliable participants in treatment, due to resistance, disciplinary actions, and other competing demands of the institutional environment.

Sechrest and Redner (1979), after closely examining the offender treatment literature, distinguished between treatment integrity and treatment strength. The term *treatment integrity* refers to what is actually delivered and is evaluated against a treatment plan that specifies what is intended. The term *treatment strength* refers to the extent to which that treatment plan itself can reasonably be expected to affect the target problem, such as delinquent behavior. Good research on delinquency treatment effects requires attention to both components.

Treatment integrity is approached within the research framework by including explicit measures of what it was that was actually delivered to each juvenile. This can be conceived as having a modality dimension and an intensity dimension. The term *modality* refers to whether the type of treatment was as planned—for example, if the treatment was behavioral contracting, was such contracting actually the predominant treatment activity in comparison, say, to eclectic counseling? The term *intensity* refers to the quantity or amount of treatment; for example, how frequently, for how many hours, over what duration? Davidson and others (forthcoming) provides a good illustration of how a researcher might check the implementation of a delinquency treatment.

Strength of treatment, however, cannot be evaluated simply by looking at what was delivered. What is required here is that a case be made for the treatment plan itself, assuming full implementation. Sechrest, West, Phillips, Redner, and Yeaton (1979) suggested a variety of ways in which the strength of the treatment plan can be assessed. One approach, of course, is to demonstrate that similar treatment has been effective against similar problems in other contexts or in other research studies. Short of that, one might rely on expert judgment, normative standards of practice, assessment of the credentials of the treatment providers, and other such tactics. Perhaps most persuasive is a close tie between the argument for the strength of the treatment and the treatment theory (discussed earlier) that gives the treatment its rationale. An adequately differentiated treatment theory should have embodied within it a framework by which treatment strength can be judged.

Treatment strength continues to be a difficult matter to judge and consequently continues to receive little explicit attention in the delinquency prevention literature. Treatment strength may ultimately have to be judged by the results. For example, as research standards and reporting improve it will be increasingly possible to use meta-analysis to assess the magnitude of effect on common measures produced by various treatments and implementation levels, for specified target juvenile groups.

Outcome Measurement. In contrast to psychotherapy, say, it would seem that delinquency treatment was blessed with a rather clear picture of the outcome variable of interest; that is, delinquent or antisocial behavior. This apparent blessing, however, is more of a curse, since delinquent or antisocial behavior cannot be easily measured. Most common is reliance on officially recorded incidents of police contact, arrest, juvenile court actions, and so on. But it is increasingly clear that these indices are not adequate. First, they are poor measures of the construct of delinquent behavior, which includes undetected as well as detected acts and excludes factors associated with police and court practices (vigilance, arrest and booking practices, and so on). Of more practical importance, perhaps, they are very insensitive as measures of potential treatment effects because of their extremely low psychometric reliability. This latter point is worth dwelling on for a moment.

It is well known that only a fraction of a juvenile's delinquent acts result in any official record or action. Williams and Gold's (1972) classic study of this, for example, found that those juveniles with arrest records were caught for only 3 percent of their chargeable actions over a three-year period. Furthermore, in only 18 percent of those cases did the apprehensions result in an entry in police arrest records. Court and probation actions, which come after arrest, can safely be assumed to occur with even lower probability. The result is that official records include an extremely large chance component—it is very much a matter of chance whether a particular delinquent act for a particular juvenile results in an official record. From a measurement standpoint, this makes such official records extremely unreliable as indexes of delinquent behavior—the same juvenile doing the same thing on two different occasions would be unlikely to produce the same "score" on the measure. I (Lipsey, 1982, 1983) estimated that the test-retest reliability of various arrest measures (frequency, severity, timing) was in the 0.20 to 0.40 range, a level far below conventional research standards. Low reliability in an outcome measure sharply reduces statistical power (Boruch and Gomez, 1977; Lipsey, 1983) and reliabilities as low as 0.20 can make even sizable treatment effects almost impossible to detect using conventional research designs and sample sizes.

Because of these and other problems with official measures (see Waldo, 1983), self-reported delinquency has become an increasingly popular approach to measuring treatment effects. Its problems are well known—questions of the accuracy of the report, social desirability response biases, sensitivity to the context of reporting (such as confidentiality), and so forth (see Hindelang, Hirschi, and Weis, 1981). The problem with this measure is that it may include too much. Juveniles, even so-called normal or nondelinquent juveniles, typically report fairly high frequencies of many delinquent behaviors. The high base rates on this measure raise the possibility that much of what it indexes may be relatively stable adolescent behavior patterns that do not sharply differentiate what we wish to identify as delinquency (or delinquents). Moreover, self-reported delinquency and official delinquency measures do not always give the same results as measures of treatment effects (see Davidson and others, 1977; forthcoming). Although it is promising, more needs to be learned about the characteristics of self-reported delinquency as a measure for indexing treatment effects.

Self-reported delinquency seems to have some potential as a delinquency measure for older juveniles, but broader measures of antisocial behavior seem to be preferred for younger juveniles. Reid, Baldwin, Patterson, and Dishion (in press) make a case for the use of observational measures for such purposes; for example, the Family Interaction Coding System, or FICS (Patterson, Ray, Shaw, and Cobb, 1969); the System for Ecological Assessment of Child Behavior Problems, or EACBP (Wahler, House, and Stambaugh, 1976); the Social Interaction Scoring System, or SISS (Conger, 1982); and the Child Behavior Checklist, or CBC (Achenbach, 1978; Achenbach and Edelbrock, 1979).

Statistical Power. The NAS report criticized the small samples prevalent in offender treatment research and the consequent lack of statistical power. It is increasingly evident that statistical power is the Achilles heel of treatment evaluation research generally and of delinquency treatment research specifically. Statistical power is the probability of detecting an effect (that is, attaining statistical significance) given that one is present. Meta-analysis results in other similar treatment areas (for example, psychotherapy) suggest that positive effects are often present and, quite likely, they are in delinquency treatment as well (Tables 1, 2, and 3). If so, the frequency of null results in evaluation research (see Rossi and Wright, 1984) may result in large part from inadequate statistical power.

As Tables 1, 2, and 3 show, available meta-analyses indicate that delinquency treatment has effect sizes in the range of 0.25 to 0.35 standard deviations. The widespread use of recidivism measures based on official records, which have low reliability and consequent insensitivity to treatment effects, may well depress these values relative to other treatment areas. The result is an exacerbated problem with statistical power. In the Wright and Dixon (1977) review of delinquency treatment, notable for its detailed summary of individual studies, the median sample size of the studies reviewed was 80. With a sample size of 80, the statistical power for detecting an effect of 0.25 standard deviations with conventional tests (for example, t-tests) and conventional alpha (0.05) would be 0.36. In other words, even if we assumed that *every* treatment produced an effect of 0.25 standard deviations superiority over the comparison group, we would find statistical significance only 36 percent of the time (Cohen, 1977).

Since the NAS report, unfortunately, there has been little evidence of increased attention to statistical power in delinquency treatment research. The nature of typical treatment circumstances and the target clientele is such that it is often difficult to increase sample size, which is the most direct route to increased statistical power. Although there are ways other than increased sample size to improve power (see Cohen, 1982; Lipsey, 1983), they have not been widely used. An interim strategy, also neglected, would be to report all significance test results as confidence intervals. In low power cases, such confidence intervals are very broad, indicating that while the statistical results are not inconsistent with the possibility of a null effect, neither are they inconsistent with the possibility of a large effect.

Research Design. The NAS report emphasized the importance of using random assignment controlled designs in offender treatment research, a standard widely acknowledged in delinquency research but more honored in the breach than in practice. Certainly the meta-analyses on delinquency treatment discussed earlier (Tables 1, 2, and 3) underscore the fallibility of the pre-/post- design that attempts to estimate treatment effects without any sort of control group at all. Two of those efforts included pre-/post- studies in their analysis, and both found that such designs yielded effect sizes grossly larger than any of the controlled designs, even those without random assignment.

Although it is increasingly common for federally funded evaluations to require randomized designs (for example, the national diversion evaluation, by Dunford, Osgood, and Weichselbaum, 1981), there have been only modest developments otherwise, none specific to the delinquency area. The mechanics of the randomization process and how its integrity can be maintained in the field has received some useful attention (Boruch and Wothke, 1985). The vexing problem of attrition, especially differential attrition from treatment and control groups has also been of interest (for example, Yeaton, Wortman, and Langberg, 1983) but seems a long way from solution.

Some of the more unusual recent cases of design innovations specifically in delinquency treatment research include (1) combining experimental studies with longitudinal studies (Patterson, 1985, 1986), (2) testing the effects of carefully defined and distinguished treatment variations rather than a single monolithic experimental treatment (Davidson and others, forthcoming), and (3) using experimental and quasi-experimental designs (for example, regression-discontinuity) in combination to strengthen the overall conclusions (Lipsey, Cordray, and Berger, 1981).

Conclusion

One chapter is closing and another is opening in the study of juvenile delinquency intervention. The 1979 and 1981 reports of the National Academy of Sciences Panel on Research on Rehabilitative Techniques concluded one chapter. The themes of that chapter were the lack of evidence for treatment efficacy, coupled with recognition that (1) the treatments that had been tried were often weak and poorly implemented and that (2) the research on them was rarely well designed for detecting any effects that might be produced.

The new chapter is opening with two important categories of developments in delinquency intervention research. First, the rise and refinement of meta-analysis permits a more thorough and precise probing of the outcomes of research, even that which falls short of ideal standards or examines weak treatments. The early evidence from meta-analysis is that even the typically low-grade research on delinquency treatment available in existing literature reveals positive treatment effects of modest, but not trivial magnitude. Second, impressive improvements in some areas of research methodology and treatment theory are enabling an increasingly high quality of research to be done on a variety of well-conceived treatment approaches. Again, the early evidence from those research programs that combine strong treatment with strong research is very encouraging even if not yet definitive.

References

Abelson, R. P. "A Variance Explanation Paradox: When a Little Is a Lot." *Psychological Bulletin,* 1985, *97,* 129-133.

Achenbach, T. M. "The Child Behavior Profile: I. Boys Aged 6-11." *Journal of Consulting and Clinical Psychology,* 1978, *46,* 478-488.

Achenbach, T. M., and Edelbrock, C. S. "The Child Behavior Profile: Boys Aged 12 to 16 and Girls Aged 6 to 11 and 12 to 16 (Vol. II)." *Journal of Consulting and Clinical Psychology,* 1979, *41,* 223-233.

Berleman, W. C. "Juvenile Delinquency Prevention Experiments: A Review and Analysis." *Reports of the National Juvenile Justice Assessment Centers.* Washington, D.C.: U.S. Department of Justice, 1980.

Boruch, R. F., and Gomez, H. "Sensitivity, Bias, and Theory in Impact Evaluations." *Professional Psychology,* 1977, *8,* 411-434.

Boruch, R. F., and Wothke, W. (eds.). *Randomization and Field Experimentation.* New Directions for Program Evaluation, no. 28. San Francisco: Jossey-Bass, 1985.

Braukman, C. J., Kirigin, K. A., and Wolf, M. M. "Group Home Treatment Research: Social Learning and Social Control Perspectives." In T. Hirschi and M. Gottfredson (eds.), *Understanding Crime: Current Theory and Research.* Newbury Park, Calif.: Sage, 1980.

Cohen, J. *Statistical Power Analysis for the Behavioral Sciences.* (rev. ed.) New York: Academic Press, 1977.

Cohen, P. "To Be or Not to Be: Control and Balancing of Type I and Type II Errors." *Evaluation and Program Planning*, 1982, *5*, 247-253.

Conger, R. D. "Social Interactional Scoring System: Observer Training Manual." Unpublished manuscript, University of Illinois, 1982.

Cullen, F. T., and Gilbert, K. E. *Reaffirming Rehabilitation*. Cincinnati, Ohio: Anderson, 1982.

Davidson, W. S., Gottschalk, R., Gensheimer, L., and Mayer, J. "Interventions with Juvenile Delinquents: A Meta-Analysis of Treatment Efficacy." Unpublished manuscript, Psychology Department, Michigan State University, 1984.

Davidson, W. S., Redner, R., Blakely, C. H., Mitchell, C. M., and Emshoff, J. G. *Diversion of Juvenile Offenders: An Experimental Comparison*. Unpublished manuscript, Psychology Department, Michigan State University, forthcoming.

Davidson, W. S., Seidman, E., Rappaport, J., Berck, P., Rapp, N., Rhodes, W., and Herring, J. "Diversion Programs for Juvenile Offenders." *Social Work Research and Abstracts*, 1977, *13*, 40-49.

Dunford, F. W., and Elliott, D. S. "Identifying Career Offenders Using Self-Reported Data." *Journal of Research in Crime and Delinquency*, 1984, *21*, 57-86.

Dunford, F. W., Osgood, D. W., and Weichselbaum, H. F. *National Evaluation of Diversion Projects: Final Report*. Boulder, Colo.: Behavioral Research Institute, 1981. (National Criminal Justice Reference Service Microfiche NCJ 80830)

Elliott, D. S., Dunford, F. W., and Huizinga, D. "The Identification and Prediction of Career Offenders Utilizing Self-Report and Official Data." In J. D. Burchard and S. N. Burchard (eds.), *The Prevention of Delinquent Behavior*. Newbury Park, Calif.: Sage, 1986.

Elliott, D. S., and Huizinga, D. "The Relationship Between Delinquent Behavior and ADM Problems." *The National Youth Survey Project Report*, no. 28. Boulder, Colo.: Behavioral Research Institute, 1984.

Flanagan, T. J., van Alstyne, D. J., and Gottfredson, M. R. *Sourcebook of Criminal Justice Statistics—1981*. Washington, D.C.: U.S. Department of Justice, 1982.

Garrett, C. J. "Meta-Analysis of the Effects of Institutional and Community Residential Treatment on Adjudicated Delinquents." Unpublished doctoral dissertation, University of Colorado, 1984.

Garrett, C. J. "Effects of Residential Treatment on Adjudicated Delinquents: A Meta-Analysis." *Journal of Research in Crime and Delinquency*, 1985, *22*, 287-308.

Gendreau, P., and Ross, B. "Effective Correctional Treatment: Bibliotherapy for Cynics." *Crime and Delinquency*, 1979, *25*, 463-489.

Glass, G. V., McGaw, B., and Smith, M. L. *Meta-Analysis in Social Research*. Newbury Park, Calif.: Sage, 1981.

Gottfredson, G. D. "A Theory-Ridden Approach to Program Evaluation: A Method for Stimulating Researcher-Implementer Collaboration." *American Psychologist*, 1984, *39*, 1101-1112.

Greenberg, D. F. "The Correctional Effects of Corrections: A Survey of Evaluations." In D. A. Greenberg (ed.), *Corrections and Punishment*. Newbury Park, Calif.: Sage, 1977.

Griffiths, D. S., and Jesness, C. *Delinquency in a Sacramento Birth Cohort*. Sacramento: California Youth Authority, 1981.

Hedges, L. V. "Distribution Theory for Glass's Estimator of Effect Size and Related Estimators." *Journal of Educational Statistics*, 1981, *6*, 107-128.

Hedges, L. V., and Olkin, I. *Statistical Methods for Meta-Analysis*. New York: Academic Press, 1985.

Hindelang, M. J., Hirschi, T., and Weis, J. G. *Measuring Delinquency*. Newbury Park, Calif.: Sage, 1981.

Hunter, J. E., Schmidt, F. L., and Jackson, G. B. *Meta-Analysis: Cumulating Research Findings Across Studies.* Newbury Park, Calif.: Sage, 1982.

Kaufman, P. "Meta-Analysis of Juvenile Delinquency Prevention Programs." Unpublished master's thesis, Claremont Graduate School, 1985.

Kirigin, K. A., Braukman, C. J., Atwater, J. D., and Wolf, M. M. "An Evaluation of the Achievement Place (Teaching Family) Group Homes for Juvenile Offenders." *Journal of Applied Behavior Analysis,* 1982, *15,* 1-16.

Lipsey, M. W. *Measurement Issues in the Evaluation of the Effects of Juvenile Delinquency Programs.* Final Report on Project 80-IJ-CX-0036, National Institute of Justice, Office of Research and Evaluation Methods, 1982. (National Criminal Justice Reference Service Microfiche NCJ 84968)

Lipsey, M. W. "A Scheme for Assessing Measurement Sensitivity in Program Evaluation and Other Applied Research." *Psychological Bulletin,* 1983, *94,* 152-165.

Lipsey, M. W. "The Paradox of Effect Size: Too Small to Detect, Too Big to Neglect." Joint meeting of the Canadian Evaluation Society, Evaluation Network, and the Evaluation Research Society, Toronto, October 1985.

Lipsey, M. W., Cordray, D. S., and Berger, D. E. "Evaluation of a Juvenile Diversion Program." *Evaluation Review,* 1981, *5,* 283-306.

Lipton, D., Martinson, R., and Wilks, J. *The Effectiveness of Correctional Treatment: A Survey of Treatment Evaluation Studies.* New York: Praeger, 1975.

Loeber, R. "The Stability of Antisocial and Delinquent Child Behavior: A Review." *Child Development,* 1982, *53,* 1431-1446.

Loeber, R., Dishion, T. J., and Patterson, G. R. "Multiple Gating: A Multistage Assessment Procedure for Identifying Youths at Risk for Delinquency." *Journal of Research in Crime and Delinquency,* 1984, *21,* 7-32.

Loeber, R., and Stouthamer-Loeber, M. "Family Factors as Correlates and Predictors of Juvenile Conduct Problems and Delinquency." In M. Tonry and N. Morris (eds.), *Crime and Justice.* Vol. 7. Chicago: University of Chicago Press, 1986.

Loeber, R., and Stouthamer-Loeber, M. "The Prediction of Deliquency." In H. C. Quay (ed.), *Handbook of Juvenile Delinquency.* New York: Wiley, in press.

Lundman, R. J., McFarlane, P. T., and Scarpitti, F. R. "Delinquency Prevention: A Description and Assessment of Projects Reported in the Professional Literature." *Crime and Delinquency,* 1976, *22,* 297-308.

Lundman, R. J., and Scarpitti, F. R. "Delinquency Prevention: Recommendations for Future Projects." *Crime and Delinquency,* 1978, *24,* 207-220.

Martin, S. E., Sechrest, L. B., and Redner, R. *New Directions in the Rehabilitation of Criminal Offenders.* Washington, D.C.: National Academy Press, 1981.

Martinson, R. "What Works? Questions and Answers About Prison Reform." *Public Interest,* 1974, *10,* 22-54.

Murray, C. *Losing Ground: American Social Policy, 1950-1980.* New York: Basic Books, 1985.

Patterson, G. R. "Beyond Technology: The Next Stage in the Development of Parent Training." In L. L'Abate (ed.), *Handbook of Family Psychology and Therapy.* Vol. 2. Homewood, Ill.: Dorsey Press, 1985.

Patterson, G. R. "Performance Models for Antisocial Boys." *American Psychologist,* 1986, *41,* 432-444.

Patterson, G. R., Chamberlain, P., and Reid, J. B. "A Comparative Evaluation of a Parent-Training Program." *Behavior Therapy,* 1982, *13,* 638-650.

Patterson, G. R., Ray, R. S., Shaw, D. A., and Cobb, J. A. *Manual for Coding of Family Interactions.* New York: Microfiche Publications, 1969.

Quay, H. C. "The Three Faces of Evaluation: What Can Be Expected to Work." *Criminal Justice and Behavior,* 1977, *4,* 341-354.
Reid, J. B., Baldwin, D. V., Patterson, G. R., and Dishion, T. J. "Some Problems Relating to the Assessment of Childhood Disorders: A Role for Observational Data." In M. Rutter, A. H. Tuma, and I. Lann (eds.), *Assessment and Diagnosis in Child and Adolescent Psychopathology.* New York: Guilford Press, in press.
Romig, D. *Justice for Our Children.* Lexington, Mass.: Lexington Books, 1978.
Rosenthal, R. *Meta-Analytic Procedures for Social Research.* Newbury Park, Calif.: Sage, 1984.
Rosenthal, R., and Rubin, D. B. "A Simple, General-Purpose Display of Magnitude of Experimental Effect." *Journal of Educational Psychology,* 1982, *74,* 166-169.
Ross, R. R., and Gendreau, P. (eds.). *Effective Correctional Treatment.* Toronto: Butterworths, 1980.
Rossi, P. H., and Wright, J. D. "Evaluation Research: An Assessment." *Annual Review of Sociology,* 1984, *10,* 331-352.
Sechrest, L., and Redner, R. "Strength and Integrity of Treatments in Evaluation Studies." In *Evaluation Reports.* Criminal Justice Evaluation Reports of the Law Enforcement Assistance Administration. Washington, D.C.: National Criminal Justice Reference Service, 1979.
Sechrest, L., West, S. G., Phillips, M. A., Redner, R., and Yeaton, W. "Some Neglected Problems in Evaluation Research: Strength and Integrity of Treatments." In L. Sechrest and others (eds.), *Evaluation Studies Review Annual.* Newbury Park, Calif.: Sage, 1979.
Sechrest, L. B., White, S. O., and Brown, E. D. *The Rehabilitation of Criminal Offenders: Problems and Prospects.* Washington, D.C.: National Academy of Sciences, 1979.
Smith, M. L., and Glass, G. V. "Meta-Analysis of Psychotherapy Outcome Studies." *American Psychologist,* 1977, *32,* 752-760.
Smith, M. L., Glass, G. V., and Miller, T. I. *The Benefits of Psychotherapy.* Baltimore, Md.: Johns Hopkins University Press, 1980.
Wahler, R. R., House, A. E., and Stambaugh, E. E., II. *Ecological Assessment of Child Problem Behaviors: A Clinical Package for Home, School, and Institutional Settings.* New York: Pergamon Press, 1976.
Waldo, G. P. (ed.). *Measurement Issues in Criminal Justice.* Newbury Park, Calif.: Sage, 1983.
Williams, J. R., and Gold, M. "From Delinquent Behavior to Official Delinquency." *Social Problems,* 1972, *20,* 209-229.
Wolf, M. M., Phillips, E. L., Fixsen, D. L., Braukmann, C. J., Kirigin, K. A., Willner, A. G., and Schumaker, J. B. "Achievement Place: The Teaching Family Model." *Child Care Quarterly,* 1976, *5,* 92-103.
Wolfgang, M. E., Figlio, R. M., and Sellin, T. *Delinquency in a Birth Cohort.* Chicago: University of Chicago Press, 1972.
Wright, W. E., and Dixon, M. C. "Community Prevention and Treatment of Juvenile Delinquency: A Review of Evaluation Studies." *Journal of Research in Crime and Delinquency,* 1977, *14,* 35-67.
Yeaton, W. H., Wortman, P. M., and Langberg, N. "Differential Attrition: Estimating the Effect of Crossovers on the Evaluation of a Medical Technology." *Evaluation Review,* 1983, *7,* 831-840.

Mark W. Lipsey is professor and chairman of the psychology program at Claremont Graduate School. He has conducted a number of evaluations of juvenile delinquency treatment programs over the last decade and is currently completing a large-scale meta-analysis of the delinquency treatment research literature.

Randomized experiments that examine the effectiveness of criminal sanctions suggest that they may increase crime, decrease crime, or have no effect. To better understand these disparate findings, we need to more carefully examine the types of sanctions being tested, in terms of their severity, certainty, and celerity (speed), and the types of offenses and offenders involved.

Randomized Experiments in Criminal Sanctions

Lawrence W. Sherman

It is over three thousand years since Daniel, in Nebuchadnezzar's court, persuaded the head guard to allow an experiment evaluating the effects of a vegetarian, teetotaling diet on the newly captive Israelites, in comparison to the meat-eating, imbibing pagans (Daniel 1: 1-15). It is exactly sixty years since R. A. Fisher (1926) substantially improved on Daniel's research design of (1) manipulation of treatment, followed by (2) observation of outcomes for inference of cause-and-effect relations, by proposing a third design element: (3) random assignment of experimental units to different treatment conditions, in order to minimize the influence of nontreatment sources of variability in outcomes. And it is almost two centuries since a philosophical revolution in criminal justice policy put the utilitarian goals of deterrence on an equal plane with retribution and just desserts.

But it is only in the last quarter-century that we have begun to combine the ideas of controlled experimentation and punishment for crime control.

The potential gains of this combination are enormous, both for

---

The comments of Howard Bloom and Michael Dennis are gratefully acknowledged.

criminological knowledge and crime control practice. As a generally nonexperimental science, criminology has developed much more slowly in the past half-century than it might have, had more experimentation been fostered. Many criminologists and policymakers have preferred the hare to the tortoise in the race for knowledge (Zimring, 1976): criminologists by making quick deductive leaps or testing multivariate models of cross-sectional data, and policymakers by relying on commonsense beliefs about what works to fight crime. Randomized experiments, in contrast, produce tiny pieces of information from which very limited conclusions should be drawn. But a gradual accumulation of experimental results over time will make a more lasting contribution to knowledge and practice.

There is no doubt that the risks are great. The random assignment of criminal sanctions is still largely uncharted in case law and potentially quite controversial. We may expect that many ongoing and future projects will fail to be implemented, that even implemented designs will be compromised, that lawsuits, union protests, or other political problems may arise. But with careful planning many of those risks can be minimized, and have been successfully avoided in a growing number of experiments. So it is now an appropriate time to review the findings they have produced to date, with their implications for future experiments.

Effects of Sanctions on Recidivism

The prevailing wisdom that punishment deters the future crimes of those punished is contradicted by the majority of the experimental evidence. My analysis of Farrington's (1983; Farrington, Ohlin, and Wilson, 1986) recent reviews shows that only the Minneapolis Domestic Assault Experiment (Sherman and Berk, 1984b) has ever found a clear deterrent effect. The isolated position of this experiment in the research literature on the specific deterrent effects in Minneapolis and the lack of them in other experiments is more likely to reflect differences in the nature of the sanction and the nature of the offense than in the city context or specific sample population.

This chapter reviews the experiments that found that sanctions make no difference in recidivism, that they increase recidivism, and that they reduce it. It takes a broad view of what constitutes sanctions, in order to better locate the theoretical context of the Minneapolis findings. It also considers the experimental evidence on interactions between types of offenders and the effects of sanctions on recidivism. The theoretical implications of the evidence are then considered for the future of specific deterrence research.

Sanctions Make No Difference. The most frequent finding from randomized experiments is that sanctions make no difference. As Farrington and others point out, however, the strength of the research design is not always matched by the strength of the sanction tested. Most of the experiments evaluated relatively weak sanctions, compared to the sudden night in jail evaluated in Minneapolis. Nonetheless, some of the experiments that found no impact examined sanctions as strong as incarceration.

It is also important to note that, unlike many evaluations, these results do not generally suffer from small sample sizes creating a bias toward the null hypothesis. The base rates of both recidivism and the sample sizes are generally adequate for moderate deterrent effects to be measurable, had they been present.

For example, Rose and Hamilton (1970) randomly assigned 200 English juvenile offenders to each of two treatments by Blackburn police. One treatment was just a caution, and the other was a caution followed by six months of police supervision. A two-year follow-up period showed no statistically significant difference in the prevalence of reoffending.

Two of the diversion experiments Farrington reviewed found no differences in recidivism. In one experiment, Byles and Maurice (1979) randomly assigned 300 apprehended juveniles to either a diversion program based on family crisis therapy or the presumably more punitive sanction of regular youth bureau processing; a two-year follow-up found no significant difference in the prevalence of recidivism. In the second and most impressive diversion experiment, Severy and Whitaker (1982) tracked 2,200 Memphis juveniles randomly assigned to juvenile court, community treatment, or no treatment; a one-year follow-up found similar recidivism rates for all three groups.

Four out of the five probation experiments Farrington reviewed found no difference in recidivism. Venezia (1972) obtained that result with a six-month follow-up of 120 California children who were designated for probation in lieu of court appearance and who were randomly assigned to either receive the probation or be released after counseling. Lichtman and Smock (1981) found no difference over two to three years follow-up with 500 male adult offenders in Detroit randomly assigned to either regular probation or twice as many contacts per month (2.4) with probation officers as in regular probation (1.3). Folkard, Smith, and Smith (1976) also doubled probation officer contact (from 1.5 monthly contacts to 3) for the intensive treatment group in a random assignment experiment with 900 adults in four areas of England. Holden (1983) found no difference in drunk driving rearrest rates over a two-year follow-up for 4,100 drivers convicted of their first drunk driving offense and randomly assigned to receive probation or not, and a therapy and education program or not.

In an experiment funded by the National Institute of Justice, New York City, Baker and Sadd (1981) randomly assigned 650 felony defendants to an experimental and a control group. The experimental group was offered job services during a four-month pretrial release period, and efforts were made by program staff to have the group's charges dismissed. The experiment succeeded in having charges dismissed against 72 percent of the experimental group, compared to the 46 percent dismissal rate for the controls. The dosage of court processing as a sanction, then, was substantially lower in the experimental group than among the controls. But a one-year follow-up period showed no difference between the groups in their rearrest rates.

Farrington also reports that three experiments involving incarceration found no differences. Lamar Empey's Provo, Utah, experiment (Empey and Erickson, 1972) was able to compare recidivism of boys randomly assigned to daily attendance at a community program under the threat of incarceration for unsatisfactory performance, or to regular probation, finding no difference in recorded offenses after four years. Empey's Silverlake experiment in Los Angeles (Empey and Lubeck, 1971) was able to compare fifteen- to seventeen-year-old boys slated for incarceration who were randomly assigned to either a community program or the incarceration, again finding no recidivism difference. Similarly, Lamb and Goertzel (1974) randomly assigned 110 California adult offenders sentenced to the county jail to either attend a community rehabilitation center or go to jail as planned. The community group had a higher rate of parole revocation over the six-month follow-up period (27 versus 17 percent), Farrington reports, but the small sample provided inadequate statistical power to ensure that the finding was not obtained by chance.

Preliminary analysis of a department store experiment in which 1,600 apprehended shoplifters were randomly assigned to be released or taken away by police (Sherman, Garten, Doi, and Miler, 1986) showed almost no difference in recidivism, either overall or among most subgroups of the sample (divided by age, race, sex, and so on).

Sanctions Increase Recidivism. Although many of the sanctions tested in random assignment experiments are indeed so weak that "no difference" results are hardly surprising, both weak and strong sanctions have had the surprising effect of increasing recidivism. Consider Farrington's (1983; Farrington, Ohlin, and Wilson, 1986, p. 76) report on a juvenile court experiment in Leeds (Berg and others, 1978; Berg, Hullin, and McGuire, 1979). Although the four other randomized experiments in probation just reviewed showed no difference, this one backfired. About a hundred children sent to court for truancy were randomly assigned to either supervision by social workers or adjournment of their cases (followed by educational welfare officers trying to get them back into school). Those "sanctioned" with continued court supervision had worse school attendance records and higher delinquency rates over a six-month follow-up than those whose cases had been adjourned.

A randomized experiment conducted by Lincoln, Klein, Teilmann, and Labin (no date) tested stronger sanctions used against more serious juvenile offenders in Los Angeles. The experiment randomly assigned apprehended juveniles to four different treatments ranked in their formality and severity: release, two types of diversion, and formal charging. The more formal and official the processing, the more frequent was the juveniles' repeat criminality over a two-year follow-up period. In another experiment with juveniles, Palmer (1974) reported that boys randomly assigned to the California Community Treatment Program in 1961–1969 were less likely to have their paroles revoked over a two-year follow-up period than those sent to an institution. Lerman (1975) has pointed out, however, that the rearrest rates for the two groups were the same, and that the parole revocation decisions may have been biased by the treatment conditions.

Preliminary analysis of an indirect experiment (Zeisel, 1968) with jail sentences for drunk drivers (Sherman, Gartin, Doi, and Miler, 1986) also suggests some enhancement of recidivism. A two-year follow-up of the driving records of some 500 drunk driving offenders found that those sentenced by a judge whose general policy was two days in jail had slightly more driving violations, although the difference was not statistically significant, than those sentenced by a judge who rarely incarcerated drunk drivers. Since the cases were assigned to the two judges at random, and almost no differences were measured in the background characteristics of the two groups, the data appear to satisfy Zeisel's standard of an indirect experiment. None of the other recidivism differences (which had lower base rates) measured were significant, but all consistently tended to show that the jail sentence produced worse driving behavior.

These results are all the more striking because they are at odds with an apparent general deterrent effect from great public visibility of a judicial "crackdown" on drunk driving. Falkowski (1984) found that monthly nighttime auto accidents declined by 20 percent over a two-year period after the crackdown began, compared to no decline in a neighboring similar county. Her findings, compared with the Sherman, Gartin, Doi, and Miler (1986) study of the same period, suggest that sanctions can have simultaneously different effects for general and specific deterrence: while punishing individual offenders may not deter them, it may deter the general population.

Some of the subgroups within a shoplifting arrest experiment (Sherman, Gartin, Doi, and Miler, 1986) also showed significantly enhanced likelihood of reoffending when they were taken away by police. Six-month recidivism rates for Roman Catholics, for example, rose from 8.7 percent among the unarrested to 15.2 percent among those arrested. Whether such differences were chance results from examining a large number of subgroups, however, is arguable.

Sanctions Deter. The experimental evidence for this proposition is the least extensive. I can find only two randomized experiments employing actual sanctions that produced specific deterrent effects. The Minneapolis domestic violence experiment (Sherman and Berk, 1984a) found that among 314 cases of misdemeanor domestic assault, those in which the offender was randomly assigned to arrest produced significantly lower prevalence and longer failure time of repeat violence than those in which the offender was assigned to the nonarrest alternative treatments, at least over a six-month follow-up period. The difference in prevalence of repeat violence was approximately a 50 percent relative reduction with arrest, from 20 to 10 percent.

A shoplifting arrest experiment (Sherman and Glick, 1982; Sherman, 1984; Sherman, Gartin, Doi, and Miler, 1986) found that among three subsamples, but not in the entire experimental sample, recidivism was deterred by arrest. These three groups may be described as "underclass" groups, since they were categorized by the store detectives as (1) "sloppy" dressers, or (2) "uncooperative" (or not scared), or (3) black. These subgroups were generally much more likely to have been handcuffed and were perhaps more likely to be treated roughly in other ways. It is not attractive to consider, but there seems to be a possibility that rough or even brutal treatment can produce a specific deterrent effect. The deterrent effects, however, were not large; the largest was a reduction of the six-month recidivism rate for sloppy dressers who were arrested, from 12.4 percent in the control group to 5.0 percent in the arrest group.

Weaker evidence of the deterrent effect of sanctions comes from several randomized tests of personalized sanction *threats.* Zimring and Hawkins (1973, p. 155) cite two in their review, and Lempert (1981-1982) contributes a third.

Zimring and Hawkins cite two studies of communications that "might influence behavior by producing the impression among members of an audience that someone is watching them personally." One was an evaluation of the Driver Improvement Meetings program in California. The program mailed offenders personal letters beginning "The records of the Department of Motor Vehicles show that you may be a negligent operator as defined by law," reminding them that their license may be suspended or revoked under certain conditions, and inviting attendance at a driver improvement meeting. The program succeeded in reducing traffic convictions for both those who attended the meetings and for those who merely received the personalized letter but failed to appear at the meeting. The results suggest that the personalized sanction threat affected driving behavior.

Zimring and Hawkins (1973, p. 155) also cite the Schwartz and Orleans (1967) field experiment on income tax compliance, calling it the best evidence on personalized sanction threats. They interpret the experiment to show that a sanction threat was not as effective as a moral appeal. But in fact the treatments in this remarkable experiment were very weak compared to what could be done, and were arguably neither a threat nor an appeal. The experiment randomly assigned almost 400 taxpayers to four groups, just before "tax time" in 1963. The "sanction threat" group received a personal survey form interview on a broad range of policy topics, including questions about punishing tax cheaters. The questions began with factual information about the certainty and severity of such punishment, such as "a jail sentence of three years could be imposed for willful failure to pay tax on interest. Under what conditions do you think the government should impose a jail sentence?" Nothing in the interview was intended to imply that the Internal Revenue Service was watching the particular subject of the interview. In that sense, the interview did not constitute a personalized threat comparable to the letter to California driving offenders. Rather, the interview was a vehicle for general communication of a sanction threat to a mass audience.

The "moral appeal" experimental group was also personally interviewed, but the special questions focused on the morality of tax cheating. The "factual" introductions listed all the good programs tax dollars paid for (hospitals, the Peace Corps) and compared tax evaders to draft dodgers (in 1963, draft dodgers were still bad people, not war protesters). A third group received a "placebo" interview with neither sanction nor morality questions, and a fourth group received no interviews at all.

IRS data showed a definite treatment effect, in which the "moral appeal" group increased its reported income and tax paid substantially over the prior year. The sanction group increased reported income by about a fourth as much—which may have been a deterrent effect against underreporting of income—but they also took more deductions, for almost no net increase in taxes paid. Schwartz and Orleans interpret this finding as possible evidence of resistance to compliance by the sanction group. Both the placebo group and the control group reported slightly less income and paid less taxes than in the prior year.

Lempert's (1981-1982) quasi-experimental evidence, in which a threatening agency was actually providing a personalized threat, shows a greater power of a sanction threat. His reanalysis of Chambers's (1979) data on compliance with orders to pay child support included a comparison of payment rates in two counties among fathers who never were arrested for failure to pay. In both counties, failure to make timely payments was followed by a letter from the Friend of the Court asking the defaulting fathers to telephone them. The message the fathers received in one county was much more severe and threatening than in the other county. These men, on average, paid 79 percent of what was due in the more threatening county and 59 percent in the less threatening county. Lempert interprets this as also being a result of the credibility of the threat from the sanctioning rates of those who fail to comply, but argues elsewhere (p. 521) that such personalized threats can be seen as an instance of specific deterrence.

These additional studies merely provide insight into specific deterrent effects. The fact remains that the Minneapolis experiment is the only one to show an across-the-board sanction effect for an entire sample.

Interaction Effects. One possible explanation for these differences in findings from different experiments is that sanctions have different effects on different kinds of offenders. It may well be that there is no one best criminal justice response to a specific offense, notwithstanding our philosophical goals of equity and just desserts (Sherman, 1984). Rather, recidivism may well be reduced most effectively by identifying a broad range of complex conditions under which different sanctions are used for different kinds of offenders committing different offenses.

Support for this view can be found in randomized experiments on correctional treatment of juveniles. Two experiments (Adams, 1970; Palmer, 1978) have found that special intensive treatments of offenders judged amenable to such treatment reduced recidivism, while such treatments *increased* the recidivism rates of offenders judged to be not amenable to such treatment. As Wilson (1983, pp. 169-170) points out, these findings are hotly disputed by Lerman and others, and they raise difficult policy implications. But the basic idea of differential reactions is strongly supported by the preliminary findings of the shoplifting arrest experiment (Sherman, Gartin, Doi, and Miler, 1986).

Theoretical Implications. Even without considering differences in offenders, it seems quite plausible that these conflicting findings are due to differences in either the nature of the sanctions or the nature of the offenses. "Sanction" is, after all, a very broad term, comparable to "medical intervention." Just as not all medical interventions are alike or equally effective against all diseases, sanctions vary widely in their qualitative characteristics as well as in the quantitative dimensions of the unpleasantness we denote as severity (length of captivity, number of parole restrictions, and so forth). The difference between, say, the findings of the Memphis drunk driving experiment (Holden, 1983) and the Minneapolis domestic violence experiment (Sherman and Berk, 1984a) may be the difference between (1) experiencing sanctions that merely interfere with how you spend your free time, and (2) being taken away to actually "do (a very short period of) time."

We also know that different offenses feature different patterns of offender careers, offender characteristics, opportunities to commit offenses, levels of commitment of the offender to criminal or to conventional social values, and other factors quite likely to affect the etiology of offending and the offender's responsiveness to sanctions. It makes sense, then, to talk not about whether sanctions deter "crime," but rather what kinds of responses to individuals are most effective in reducing recidivism for particular kind of crimes. As Lempert (1981-1982) observes, our knowledge is more likely to accumulate in a theoretically productive way if we attend to such differences.

If we set aside the enormous differences in the nature of both the offenses and the sanctions, could anything else explain the deterrent effects they produced? The answer may be related to the prior sanctioning of the offender for the specific offense.

We know that in the Minneapolis experiment only 5 percent of the offenders showed a prior arrest for domestic assault, despite a 59 percent prevalence of prior arrest for any offense and 31 percent for crimes against people (Sherman and Berk, 1984a, p. 266). If the spouse assaulters were being punished for the first time for an offense that they had committed and perhaps even been caught at before, then it may have had the effect of substantially increasing their estimates of the certainty of punishment and the estimated costs of the offense.

We cannot, of course, actually ignore the differences in the nature of sanctions across all these experiments. Perhaps something that distinguishes arrest in Minneapolis from other sanctions produced such different findings. One possibility is the extended time in police custody attached to the arrest. All the arrested offenders in Minneapolis spent at least one night in jail, while others spent even more time.

If initial time in custody at arrest (for nonserious offenders) makes more difference than extended incarceration many weeks after the crime (Empey and Lubeck, 1971; Lamb and Goertzel, 1974), a theory of sanctions must reconcile such findings with the traditional assumption of inverse relations of severity and recidivism. Although greater amounts of incarceration may reduce recidivism, other things being equal (at least in theory), the *speed* ("celerity") of punishment may alter the effects of severity. That is, the value of severity may be conditioned on its celerity. The longer the time lapse between the offense (or the official detection of the offense) and the incarceration, the less effect the severity of the incarceration may have on the offender's recidivism rate.

Why should that be so? Consider the suddenness and surprise that arrest must produce, especially for offenses with low certainty of apprehension. If one has made plans for the next several hours or days, even for sheer hedonism like dating or going to sports events, the unexpected interruption of those plans for a period of incarceration can be quite painful and disruptive. Postadjudication incarceration, in contrast, comes only after a long period of time (if at all) during which the offender is gradually accustomed to the possibility, developing expectations of exactly how long the incarceration may last, and making life plans accordingly. Extended incarceration at time of arrest is a much greater violation of expectations than it is after sentencing. Given recent psychological findings about the importance of expectations in mental health, it is plausible to argue that greater violations of expectations cause greater suffering.

This theoretical argument, and not any substantive differences in the nature of the offense or the offender population, might explain why one night in jail in Minneapolis deterred spouse assault, but two nights in jail in Minneapolis failed to deter drunk driving. The drunk drivers had ample notice at sentencing of when they actually had to serve their time, and were often incarcerated on weekends to minimize the disruption of their employment and other aspects of life. A policy of two days in jail had been widely publicized by the local judiciary, and drunk driving offenders had little apparent reason to have their expectations violated. The spouse assailants, in contrast, had no reason to believe that they would be arrested, since most of them had experienced police intervention in the past without being arrested. Then, suddenly, without any publicity or notice about a change in policy, they were arrested and incarcerated.

This argument may shed additional light on the relationship between general and specific deterrence. As Lempert (1981-1982) observes, the two kinds of deterrence are different kinds of concepts rather than two sides of the same coin, but they interact in important and complex ways. First, specific deterrence can affect general deterrence. To the extent that a small group of high-rate offenders account for a substantial portion of all crime committed in a population (for example, Wolfgang, Figlio, and Sellin, 1972; Greenwood, 1982), specific deterrence of those offenders can exercise a major influence on the population crime rate. Second, as Zimring and Hawkins (1973) note, sanctioning of individuals enhances the credibility of the threat associated with the general command not to break the law, thereby increasing general deterrent effects on the population of sanctioned criminals. It is therefore "possible that the individual deterrence of persons actually punished accounts for a considerable portion of the negative association between crime rate and certainty of punishment that is typically interpreted as evidence of general deterrence" (Lempert, 1981-1982, p. 515).

Second, general deterrence can affect specific deterrence. The prevalence and incidence of recidivism among offenders sanctioned in varying ways may be conditioned by the credibility with which those offenders perceive the general command, and the population rates of certainty, celerity, and severity of punishment per offense that sanctioned offenders perceive. The greater the punishment risks for the general population, the greater the specific deterrent effects of punishment may be.

But if the expectation argument is extended further, a "contrarian" effect may be at work: specific deterrence is enhanced to the extent that it violates offender expectations (in a direction of more severity) based on perceptions of population or community rates of sanctioning.

And if that argument is correct, we may expect arrests of spouse assaulters to have a greater specific deterrent effect in communities where arrests for that offense are rare (as they were in Minneapolis) than in communities where such arrests are more common—as they are becoming in many more communities (Sherman and Hamilton, 1984; Sherman and Cohn, 1986).

Quite apart from the expectation argument about *deterrence*, the amount of time spent in police custody at arrest may have an important *incapacitation* effect for offenses entailing emotional arousal and anger at the complainant. Spouse assault, for example, is often committed while offenders are intoxicated or using drugs, which can reduce emotional control to facilitate the offense, and can enhance the level of anger at the victim for helping to precipitate the arrest. Although this is unlikely to be a problem with shoplifting, domestic violence arrests may require extended police custody in order to provide time for both the adrenalin of anger and blood alcohol or drug content to subside. Otherwise, the offender may return from police custody directly to the victim and do even greater violence.

Conclusion

In summary, this review of the general experimental literature on the effects of sanctions on recidivism produces several concrete implications for the design of future randomized experiments on criminal sanctions.

First, the amount of lapsed time between the offense and the imposition of the sanction is a potentially crucial determinant of the effectiveness of the sanction, and deserves high priority in future tests.

Second, the dosage of a sanction, such as the length of time in police custody attendant to an arrest, may also be extremely important, both theoretically and practically. Determining its impact on both short- and long-term recidivism should be a high priority for future research.

Third, there seems to be a substantial possibility of interaction effects between sanctions and type of offender. Prior offending, in particular, may be quite powerful in mediating the impact of the sanction. Although no such interaction effect was detected in Minneapolis, the sample sizes were insufficient to treat that finding as conclusive. The shoplifting results suggest that interactions might be important. Thus, sufficient sample sizes for these and other possible interaction effects should be given a high priority for future experiments.

Fourth, there may also be an interaction effect between the sanctioning of individual offenders and recent publicity or other sources of perceptions about general community policy toward any specific kind of crime. Communities with higher levels of sanctioning for that offense may show less specific deterrence of those who are actually sanctioned, even though they may be obtaining general deterrence of that offense by sanctioning those less specifically deterrable offenders; the Minneapolis drunk driving studies of general deterrent and specific deterrent effects of the same sanctions support this hypothesis.

These and other issues can only be addressed by gathering more findings from more randomized experiments. In addition to replicating key experiments (as the Minneapolis domestic violence experiment is being replicated in six sites), we need to continue to expand our scope of randomized tests of experiments to more types of offenses, offenders, and sanctions. Induction from these results, rather than deduction from grand theory,seems the best way to improve our knowledge of effective use of sanctions.

References

Adams, S. "The PICO Project." In N. Johnston, L. Savitz, and M. Wolfgang (eds.), *The Sociology of Punishment and Correction*. New York: Wiley, 1970.

Baker, S. H., and Sadd, S. *Diversion of Felony Arrests*. Washington, D.C.: National Institute of Justice, 1981.

Berg, I., Consterdine, M., Hullin, R., McGuire, R., and Tyrer, S. "The Effect of Two Randomly Allocated Court Procedures on Truancy." *British Journal of Criminology*, 1978, *18*, 232-244.

Berg, I., Hullin, R., and McGuire, R. "A Randomly Controlled Trial of Two Court Procedures in Truancy." In D. P. Farrington, K. Hawkins, and S. Lloyd-Bostock (eds.), *Psychology, Law, and Legal Processes*. London: Macmillan, 1979.

Berk, R. A., and Sherman, L. W. "Police Responses to Family Violence Incidents: An Analysis of an Experimental Design with Incomplete Randomization." *Journal of the American Statistical Association*, in press.

Byles, J. A., and Maurice, A. "The Juvenile Services Project: An Experiment in Delinquency Control." *Canadian Journal of Criminology*, 1979, *21*, 155-165.

Chambers, D. *Making Fathers Pay: The Enforcement of Child Support*. Chicago: University of Chicago Press, 1979.

Cook, T. D., and Campbell, D. T. *Quasi-Experimentation: Design and Analysis Issues for Field Settings*. Chicago: Rand-McNally, 1979.

Empey, L. T., and Erickson, M. L. *The Provo Experiment*. Lexington, Mass.: Heath, 1972.

Empey, L. T., and Lubeck, S. G. *The Silverlake Experiment*. Chicago: Aldine, 1971.

Falkowski, C. L. "The Impact of Two-Day Jail Sentences for Drunk Drivers in Hennepin County, Minnesota, Final Report." Contract Number DTNH22-8-05110. Washington, D.C.: U.S. Department of Transportation, National Highway Traffic Safety Administration, 1984.

Farrington, D. P. "Randomized Experiments on Crime and Justice." In M. Tonry and N. Morris (eds.), *Crime and Justice: An Annual Review of Research*. Vol. 4. Chicago: University of Chicago Press, 1983.

Farrington, D. P., Ohlin, L., and Wilson, J. Q. *Understanding and Controlling Crime*. New York: Springer-Verlag, 1986.

Federal Judicial Center. *Experimentation and the Law.* Washington, D.C.: Federal Judicial Center, 1981.

Fisher, R. A. "The Arrangement of Field Experiments." *Journal of the Ministry of Agriculture, Great Britain,* 1926, *33,* 503-513.

Folkard, M. S., Smith, D. E., and Smith, D. D. *Impact.* Vol. 2. London: H. M. Stationery Office, 1976.

Greenwood, P. *Selective Incapacitation.* Santa Monica, Calif.: The Rand Corporation, 1982.

Holden, R. T. "Rehabilitative Sanctions for Drunk Driving: An Experimental Evaluation." *Journal of Research in Crime and Delinquency,* 1983, *20,* 55-72.

Lamb, H. R., and Goertzel, V. "Ellsworth House: A Community Alternative to Jail." *American Journal of Psychiatry,* 1974, *131,* 64-68.

Lempert, R. "Organizing for Deterrence: Lessons from a Study of Child Support." *Law and Society Review,* 1981-1982, *16,* 513-568.

Lempert, R. "From the Editor." *Law and Society Review,* 1983, *18,* 5-10.

Lerman, P. *Community Treatment and Social Control.* Chicago: University of Chicago Press, 1975.

Lichtman, C. M., and Smock, S. M. "The Effects of Social Services on Probationer Recidivism: A Field Experiment." *Journal of Research in Crime and Delinquency,* 1981, *18,* 81-100.

Lincoln, S. B., Klein, M. W., Teilmann, K. S., and Labin, S. "Control Organizations and Labeling Theory: Official Versus Self-Reported Delinquency." Unpublished manuscript, Department of Sociology, University of Southern California, n.d.

Palmer, T. B. "The Youth Authority's Community Treatment Project." *Federal Probation,* 1974, *38,* 3-14.

Palmer, T. B. *Correctional Intervention and Research.* Lexington, Mass.: Lexington Books, 1978.

Rose, G., and Hamilton, R. A. "Effects of a Juvenile Liaison Scheme." *British Journal of Criminology,* 1970, *10,* 2-20.

Schwartz, R. D., and Orleans, S. "On Legal Sanctions." *University of Chicago Law Review,* 1967, *34,* 274-300.

Sechrest, L., White, S. O., and Brown, E. D. (eds.). *The Rehabilitation of Criminal Offenders: Problems and Prospects.* Washington, D.C.: National Academy of Sciences, 1979.

Severy, L. J., and Whitaker, J. M. "Juvenile Diversion: An Experimental Analysis of Effectiveness." *Evaluation Review,* 1982, *6,* 753-774.

Sherman, L. W. "Experiments in Police Discretion: Scientific Boon or Dangerous Knowledge?" *Law and Contemporary Problems,* 1984, *47* (4), 61-81.

Sherman, L. W., with E. E. Hamilton. "The Impact of the Minneapolis Domestic Violence Experiment: Wave 1 Findings." Washington, D.C.: Police Foundation, 1984.

Sherman, L. W., and Berk, R. A. *The Minneapolis Domestic Violence Experiment.* Washington, D.C.: Police Foundation, 1984a.

Sherman, L. W., and Berk, R. A. "The Specific Deterrent Effects of Arrest for Domestic Assault." *American Sociological Review,* 1984b, *49,* 261-272.

Sherman, L. W., and Cohn, E. G., with E. E. Hamilton. "Police Policy on Domestic Violence." Crime Control Reports no. 1. Washington, D.C.: Crime Control Institute, 1986.

Sherman, L. W., Gartin, P. R., Doi, D., and Miler, S. "The Effects of Jail Time on Drunk Drivers." Presentation to the American Society of Criminology, Atlanta, Ga., November 1986.

Sherman, L. W., and Glick, B. D. "The Specific Deterrent Effects of Arrest: A Field Experiment." Proposal submitted to the National Institute of Justice, Police Foundation, Washington, D.C., 1982.
Venezia, P. S. "Unofficial Probation: An Evaluation of Its Effectiveness." *Journal of Research in Crime and Delinquency*, 1972, *9*, 149-170.
Wilson, J. Q. *Thinking About Crime.* New York: Basic, 1983.
Wolfgang, M. E., Figlio, R. M., and Sellin, T. *Delinquency in a Birth Cohort.* Chicago: University of Chicago Press, 1972.
Zeisel, H. "The Indirect Experiment." *Law and Society Review*, 1968, *2*, 504-508.
Zimring, F. E. "Field Experiments in General Deterrence: Preferring the Tortoise to the Hare." *Evaluation*, 1976, *3*, 132-135.
Zimring, F. E., and Hawkins, G. J. *Deterrence: The Legal Threat in Crime Control.* Chicago: University of Chicago Press, 1973.

Lawrence W. Sherman is professor of criminology, University of Maryland, and president, Crime Control Institute, Washington, D.C. He has designed and directed fourteen field experiments in criminal justice, police practices, and sanctions, including the 1984 Minneapolis domestic violence experiment. He is currently directing a large-scale replication of that experiment in Minneapolis.

The course of evaluation in mental health has been altered by the sociopolitical context of the 1970s and 1980s. Among the lessons learned are (1) the limitations of some evaluation technologies, (2) improvements that have occurred in others, and (3) the need for "echelon-specific" evaluations. Insufficient recognition has been given to the need for both internal and external evaluation and replication.

Mental Health Program Evaluation and Needs Assessment

James A. Ciarlo, Charles Windle

The field of mental health program evaluation has grown rapidly over the past two decades, with an expanding literature that shows few signs of topping out. The context of evaluation activities has changed sharply, however; decreased federal support of service programs has weakened demands for local or federal evaluation. But the field seems still to be developing, and new evaluation opportunities may be emerging from the need for better information to improve the efficiency and effectiveness of current service programs.

The changed context makes this an opportune time to review the major developments in the field of evaluation, both to orient newcomers and to reorient experienced evaluators who have become highly specialized or committed to particular approaches. This overview supplements and updates earlier presentations of mental health evaluation activities, including Coursey and others, *Program Evaluation for Mental Health* (1977); Attkisson, Hargreaves, Horowitz, and Sorensen, *Evaluation of Human Service Programs* (1978); and Stahler and Tash, *Innovative Approaches to Mental Health Evaluation* (1982). We will also take a more historical perspective, reflecting the social contexts that shaped mental health program evaluation, and highlighting developments that seem significant from the vantage points of a former local agency evaluator and investigator on several evaluation-oriented grant projects (Ciarlo) and an evaluator of federal programs and monitor of many federal evaluation grants and contracts (Windle). We share a public health orientation, placing priority on benefits for people who need services, on improvement of programs, and on overall accountability to the general public; we are less concerned with routine information needs of the service system bureaucracy or "system maintenance" requirements. Our review is thus weighted toward the former perspectives.

The Primary Context of Evaluation—Federal and State-Supported Programs

Mental health evaluation activity was strongly stimulated and shaped during the 1970s by the federal Community Mental Health Centers (CMHCs) program, and afterward by federal and state service initiatives for the chronically mentally ill (and most recently, the homeless mentally ill). We highlight some specific evaluation concepts and tools that have been shaped by these environments.

State Mental Hospitals and Associated Programs. One of the earliest evaluation-related developments, the implementation of management information systems (MISs), had its roots in attempts to more accurately describe the operation of large state hospital programs. In the 1960s, the National Institute of Mental Health (NIMH) funded a number of efforts to better define mental health admission problems, treatment events, and patient improvement. A hospital-oriented paradigm of sequential admission-treatment-discharge events strongly influenced the structure of early service program data systems and associated data capture forms, from the card-based client data system at Fort Logan Hospital in Colorado to the Rockland, New York, multistate information system adopted by a number of states. Computer technology was felt to make possible rapid feedback of information about admissions, discharges, and patient flow data, so that administrators and clinicians would make better-informed decisions and improve system functioning. Psychiatric case registers for states and counties were also established, although primarily for research rather than evaluation purposes. This federal effort to improve data collection and use has continued, with increasing recognition of the difficulties in absorbing and applying such information; this trend, in turn, has affected how program evaluators routinely function. Quantitative description and monitoring of changes in service operations have become major components of agency-based evaluator roles. In addition, continuing improvement of data systems at many agencies has made possible more sophisticated evaluation studies, such as determining the relative accessibility of services to community subgroups. It appears to us that the basic foundation of most local- and state-level evaluation activity is still the agency-based, services-oriented management information system, and its employment in basic administrative reporting and decision making.

The Community Mental Health Centers (CMHCs) Program. The CMHC program (1963-1980) gave a huge impetus to program evaluation because requirements for program accountability were directly included in the federal legislation. Five major forms of evaluation were eventually required as the program's legislative mandate developed, all attempting to solve observed problems with the program as implemented. A sixth was in the process of being implemented under the Mental Health Systems Act of 1980 as the federally supported CMHC era ended. Each is briefly described here.

CMHC Self-Evaluation. The first impetus came from the law specifying "research and evaluation" as a service that qualified for federal staffing grant support. More stimulus was provided by the amendments of 1975 (PL 94-63), which required each CMHC to expend at least 2 percent of its budget on self-evaluation. As a result, a large number of people were soon employed as evaluators, and got firsthand experience in applying research methods to practical, administrative problems under field conditions. This experience, with its mixture of program advocacy, accountability, and the search for truth—coupled with frequent evaluator frustration at the lack of significant impact on the programs themselves—substantially influenced mental health evaluators. Academically originated commitment to doing well-controlled studies and costly, thorough client assessments often gave way to quick data analyses for producing reports useful to administrators, and sometimes even direct involvement in decision-making committees. Later, with the elimination of the federal requirement for self-evaluation (see later), CMHCs often "reorganized" this evaluation function, combining it with other activities such as administration and fiscal operations (Larsen and Jerrell, 1986). Thus, this form of self-evaluation seems to have earned "intermediate" marks at best from local administrators.

External, Oversight Evaluation. Like several other federal programs, the CMHC program was required to set aside 1 percent of its funds for evaluation by the U.S. Department of Health and Human Services. This activity was conducted under contracts to non-CMHC organizations and focused on service process goals of the CHMC program (Feldman and Windle, 1973). These evaluations, although their results seem relevant to improving the CMHC program, actually had little impact on program oversight by the federal executive branch or the states, or on self-improvement actions by the CMHCs. However, the results of these evaluations were used as evidence of the CMHC program's strengths and weaknesses in later evaluative studies done by the U.S. General Accounting Office (for example, U.S. General Accounting Office, 1977) and the Nader group's report on CMHCs (Chu and Trotter, 1974), and thus indirectly guided Congressional efforts to improve the program through legislation.

External, Adversarial Evaluation. Evaluations by agencies removed from the direct management of the CMHC program, such as the U.S. General Accounting Office, and especially the evaluation by the consumer interest-oriented Nader organization just noted, played an important part in shaping the CMHC program. Although their evaluations were criticized for lack of scientific methods or a too-narrow scope, the reports of these evaluations were attended to by Congress and the federal CMHC program staff, with consequent changes introduced into the legislation.

Citizen-Consumer Evaluation. Although the CMHC amendments of 1975 explicitly mandated a role for residents of each CMHC's catchment area in the evaluations required of each CMHC, this requirement was generally ignored by the local programs (Flaherty and Olsen, 1978). CMHC staff regarded this requirement as of little value, and the few other residents of CMHC catchment areas who learned of the requirement did not mount significant pressure for CMHC compliance.

Peer Review for Quality Assurance. By the late 1970s it appeared that quality assurance (QA) procedures, including formal peer review and utilization review, were becoming key CMHC evaluation activities. A widely distributed NIMH publication detailed the goals and procedures for quality assurance (Werlin, 1976), and related chapters in evaluation texts (for example, Woy, Lund, and Attkisson, 1978) reflected rapid development in this area. This development paralleled federal legislation mandating peer review and utilization review for federally reimbursed medical services. Currently, however, interest in CMHC peer review systems seems to be generated and sustained primarily by third-party reimbursors and the Joint Commission on Accreditation of Hospitals (JCAH), whose "accreditation" can improve facilities' chances for services reimbursement by third-party payors. Flaherty and Olsen's (1978) study of CMHC evaluation activities concluded that, although QA activities had not apparently improved services, the approach did hold promise because of its connection to third-party reimbursement plans. Two more recent studies that formally evaluated the impact of peer review systems on services, using control groups and a prospective study design (Sinclair and Frankel, 1982; Ray and others, 1986), found that some benefit to services was indeed attributable to QA procedures.

Program Performance Measurement. The notion of management by objectives, developed outside the mental health field, gradually exerted a strong influence on evaluation thinking and strategy, and eventually culminated in a formal procedure (discussed later) for linking evaluation of program achievements to measures of specific objectives. The system of measures and monitoring of changes in those measures was aptly termed "performance measurement," and such systems have been used in evaluation at the national, state, and even local levels. In the final years of the CMHC program, NIMH was beginning to apply an operations management system (OMS) of program performance measures to the CMHC program (Jacobs and Thompson, 1986). These measures included indicators of efficiency in service delivery, volume of services provided to different target groups, and productivity ratios such as client caseload per clinician. In fact, the Mental Health Systems Act of 1980 (PL 96-398) adopted this approach as the key evaluation mechanism to ensure CMHC accountability. This performance measurement system had barely begun to be disseminated to CMHCs, and limited implementation started, when the federal oversight role for CMHCs was terminated. However, very similar versions of this system have survived in some states, and also in many local CMHCs that are members of the National Council of Community Mental Health Centers (Sorensen, Zelman, Hanbery, and Kucic, 1986). Under these systems, CMHCs are able to compare their own performance data (usually related to service processes or efficiency) against data from other facilities compiled by their states or the NCCMHC.

Other evaluation techniques besides these six, of course, were used in mental health program evaluation work, such as client outcome assessment and community needs assessment. Many of these others were quite "generic," however, and not specifically products of the CMHC program. We cover them in another section.

The Federal Community Support Program. The small federal Community Support Program originated largely in response to the failure of the CMHC program to serve many of the chronically mentally ill, who become more visible with deinstitutionalization, or release from the state hospitals back into the larger community (Windle and Scully, 1976; Chu and Trotter, 1974; U.S. General Accounting Office, 1977). This program had an impact on evaluation methodology through its focus on structural arrangements among service facilities to coordinate the services of many different agencies that are necessary to meet the multiple needs of the chronically ill. Thus, measures of interorganizational relations have been reviewed (Morrissey, Hall, and Lindsey, 1982), and the most promising of these field-tested (Morrissey, Tausig, and Lindsey, 1985). A new private foundation initiative in improving services to the chronically mentally ill focuses on organizational arrangements in service delivery, such as centralization of authority and coordination of diverse services (Aiken, Somers, and Shore, 1986). In addition, recordkeeping and records coordination procedures may need to be revised so that agency MISs can generate compatible client information and services data. In contrast to the CMHC arena, evaluation opportunities in this service context may be increasing as more states focus services on more seriously disabled clients, both in residential and community contexts.

Program Evaluation and Services Research in Mental Health: Some Metaissues

Next we shift our perspective from the sociopolitical context of evaluation to its *professional* context. We attach the fashionable prefix *meta*, "higher," to the rather prosaic term *issues*, to suggest that these topics represent some "higher order" ideas that have been developed in the formal evaluation literature, or have emerged from evaluation practice.

Knowledge-Oriented Research Versus Decision-Focused Evaluation. It has become customary to try to give evaluation a special place in the behavioral sciences, based on the primary purpose and usual setting of an evaluation study. The distinction usually made is that, in contrast to most research (including research on mental health services), evaluation studies are *always* addressed primarily to nonresearchers and nonevaluators (such as service program managers, funding agencies and legislatures, and other "stakeholders"); and are *always* focused on actual or potential decisions about a specific program. A stint of service in an agency evaluator position may be needed to deepen one's appreciation of the difference between independently conducted research and agency evaluation chores, but we believe the distinction is real. Practicing evaluators try to focus on topics directly relevant to a decision about the program being evaluated, especially if the decision is aimed at supporting or improving the program. It is rare, though, for them to address cutting the program back, or terminating it altogether, since such decisions are difficult to influence because of political factors and the enduring views of those who initially helped to create or implement the program. But, in general, a decision orientation is the key feature of program evaluation.

However, contributions to theory or generalizable knowledge that are produced by service researchers who try to develop theory or explicate the relationships among variables, or by clinically oriented people seeking to advance treatment effectiveness, have the potential for stimulating changes in *multiple* program settings, and are therefore considered more prestigious by most professionals. Research increases our knowledge base, independently of whether the study results are noted by local service program managers. Unfortunately, program managers read little formal services research literature, and hence remain largely ignorant of it. But despite the well-known time pressures on managers and the low relevance of some formal services research, we believe that the body of published services research should be considered, along with local evaluation products in program decision making. Some of this literature *is* relevant to many mental health programs, and program evaluators may be key people in bringing formal services research findings to the attention of program officials and policymakers—not by *doing* such research, but by *being aware* of it and telling managers of its relevance to decisions.

The two endeavors, however, are often closely linked. Rossi (1978) has argued that after service researchers test the validity of service concepts, there is still need to test the feasibility of practical application, and then assess whether these services are actually applied in programs so that the desirable results originally found can occur. This latter step involves the assessing of service *processes* by evaluators, which is usually simpler than studying client outcomes as required for validating service concepts. When fairly well routinized, service process evaluation can take the form of "performance measurement" (described earlier).

However, James Ciarlo (the first author of this chapter) has argued for inclusion of actual client impact, or outcome studies, as a key part of evaluation, at least at the state level (Ciarlo, 1982). Studies have shown that program funders want some idea of the actual benefits to clients, especially in relation to the resources expended; this can most credibly be done with good client outcome studies. And since the primary purpose is to inform and satisfy the program funders, the activity still qualifies as evaluation rather than services research. Furthermore, distinctions between research and program evaluation blur in evaluations of large-scale programs (where service processes may be considered variables), and in some small experiments (where certain controls or conditions are of only parochial interest). Probably a better distinction between research and program evaluation rests on whom the investigator is trying to serve, and the roles adopted for that purpose.

Roles of the Evaluator-Researcher. Listed here are several roles that people hired as program evaluators may play. The first role flows from the remarks just made, and the remaining four were listed in a review of general evaluation theory and practice by Cook and Shadish (1986):

1. Independent researcher-scholar
2. Information broker
3. Servant to the administrator
4. Educator of stakeholders
5. Consultant to consumers.

In our experience, most front-line evaluators in mental health agencies do not act as independent researcher-scholars. The major exception occurs when an external funding source invites an evaluator to conduct a piece of research of no real interest to the program manager, apart from the prestige of having funded research within the agency. Some of Ciarlo's work fits this role quite well, and it seems to have had less impact on the programs he was evaluating than did his less scholarly activities, such as gathering and presenting service statistics to key audiences.

The second role—information broker—is more common, with the evaluator being viewed as someone who knows many things managers think they need to know to make informed decisions—what the legislature is likely to want in the way of state-funded services next year, or how the agency's caseload compares to that of competitor agencies.

Most local agency program evaluators act primarily in terms of the third role, doing those data-oriented tasks or studies the manager wants. This role can be powerful when the manager believes in the importance of data for decision making, trusts evaluators, and relies on their input to key decisions. In Rich's (1981) conception of the bureaucratic knowledge utilization process, it is the "trusted aide" who most often persuades the executive to adopt or reject some program alteration, particularly when the consequences are not entirely known, as is the case with most crucial decisions. Since trust is the key to this role, it may also be achieved by personal relationships, affection, and loyalty, rather than by good ideas and careful work; in such instances, much of the potential worth of program evaluation itself may be lost. Unfortunately, this role can also easily be converted into less evaluative ones—data processor, billing system operator, program advocate, or program publicist. Only a little selective reporting is needed to move one out of the role of objective evaluator to program advocate, and pressure from above for such selection is common. It is a fortunate evaluator whose employer expects him or her to play the role of objective information-gatherer and interpreter, particularly in areas in which the program is *not* accomplishing its stated or expected functions.

The role we have seen played least is the consumer consultant role, although there were aspects of this role in the evaluations funded in the late 1960s and early 1970s under the federally funded Model Cities programs. In Denver, and possibly other cities with such programs, politically active citizen "advisory" groups had direct access to evaluators, whose job included advice about the overall quality and functioning of funded programs. On a larger scale, the early CMHC program evaluation done by the Nader group (Chu and Trotter, 1974) provided useful (and critical) information to the public. The viability of this role undoubtedly depends on the strength of the relevant consumer group and its success in demanding (or paying for) evaluations. Since mental health clients (consumers) are not a strong force, either locally or nationally, the consumer consultant role is rare in mental health. Of course, some evaluations from a consumer perspective, done by consumers themselves, are available; and while additional face validity and political clout may be gained via such authorship, methodological sophistication is often lost (Bradley, Allard, and Mulkern, 1984).

Also infrequent is the role of educator of stakeholders. Exceptions are evaluators being called on to explain program data in legislative hearings, or to be an expert witness in lawsuits alleging the inadequacy of services or impropriety of application of program funds. Experience suggests that a successful evaluator probably adopts different roles specific to circumstances, and/or blends roles in ways compatible with both the environment and the evaluator's interpersonal style and motivations—for example, to be a "team player," "hard-nosed scientist," or "power behind the throne." Many local and state-level evaluation positions seem flexible enough to allow expression of many inner self-images. Although this flexibility may not foster a strong professional image (such as that enjoyed by Certified Public Accountants), it does allow evaluation activity to survive under a variety of circumstances. And there does seem to exist, particularly in the developing standards for evaluators, a basic commitment to the independent scholar role as "teller of truth," and (at least in the public sector) the role of advocate for the public interest. From these two evaluation roles, a recognized profession may yet emerge.

Evaluating Goals and Objectives Versus "Value-Free" Evaluation. Weiss (1977), Scriven (1983), and others have argued that we should not make serious attempts to evaluate the degree to which formally stated program goals or objectives are being achieved, on the grounds that such goals are often vague, contradictory, and not the real ones anyway. Proposed alternatives to evaluating programs by formal goals and objectives include (1) studying factors one guesses will be relevant to future decisions, (2) examining theory-based hypotheses about how services are expected to affect program or client outcomes, and (3) performing primarily descriptive studies of changes in programs and clientele. These alternatives should all be considered, since mental health programs have a tradition of *not* having clear, precisely defined objectives with accepted, operationally defined measures of accomplishment for these objectives. Yet by *not* focusing on a program's achievements in terms of its publicly stated objectives, the evaluator fails to meet a basic responsibility for clear, truthful communication to the funding agency and the public, as well as to the program managers themselves. In fact, a main benefit of program evaluation is that it forces people to think realistically about program processes and outcomes. Overt program objectives are an excellent source of leverage to stimulate program change, by revealing discrepancies between idealized goals and actual achievements. Being a catalyst for improving services is perhaps the most important contribution that evaluators can make.

Internal Versus External Evaluation. In mental health, the internal-external evaluation debate arose primarily in the context of the CMHC program. It experienced the tension between these approaches at two levels—the overall national program, and the individual CMHCs. External CMHC evaluations of the national program were done by the Nader group (Chu and Trotter, 1974) and by the GAO (for example, U.S. General Accounting Office, 1977); these seem to have had considerable influence on Congress, which continued to legislate changes addressed to program shortcomings. Internal evaluations at this level, intended primarily for use by NIMH, were done through contracts planned and monitored by NIMH. These studies, while internal, still appeared to allow sufficient objectivity for critical findings to be developed, and they were fairly widely disseminated within the CMHC program. Unfortunately, both the amount of publicity given to these evaluative studies, and subsequent use of their results by NIMH, were disappointing. Some of these results were, however, incorporated into the GAO reports, where they probably helped to influence Congress to mandate changes. Yet these often critical GAO reports, seen as external by NIMH, were still viewed by some as reflecting Congress's own internal commitment to the CMHC program (Siegel and Doty, 1978) and as not sufficiently challenging its entire structure.

At the local CMHC level, most internal evaluation activities, even though quantitative, were mainly descriptive and seldom challenged the CMHC's performance. Judgments of the success of such self-evaluation efforts were mixed; some writers (for example, Cook and Shadish, 1982; Windle, 1983) were highly critical of the local evaluations funded under the 2 percent evaluation requirement, although they did not review these systematically nor directly compare their results to external or centrally funded evaluations. Others (such as Ciarlo, 1983; Kirkhart, 1983) were more optimistic about what was accomplished at the local level by internal evaluators, stressing the greater local relevance of these activities, and the opportunity for inserting evaluation findings into local decision making, in which evaluators often participated. Other individual CMHC program evaluation activities were external—quality assurance activities by regional panels of professional peers, a very few evaluations done in response to the mandated involvement of citizens in CMHC evaluation, and routine monitoring (often, annual site visits) by federal and state staff.

The effectiveness and appropriateness of either type in the mental health context is not easy to resolve. The issue was debated in an issue of *Evaluation and Program Planning* (Neigher and others, 1983), but no clear conclusion was reached. We (the authors of this chapter) diverged in our assessments, one endorsing primarily local internal evaluation (Ciarlo) and the other preferring a redirection of both local and national-level evaluation resources to mental health issues broader than even the CMHC program (Windle). It is clear that two of the external forms of CMHC evaluation—citizen-involved evaluation and professional peer review—had little impact on CMHCs during the 1970s, largely because they were never seriously implemented on a large scale (Flaherty and Olsen, 1978). Another form, the monitoring of CMHCs by government oversight groups, was resented by many CMHCs, and was also regarded by the monitoring staff as having less influence than desired on CMHC programs; a few exceptions, involving threatened suspension of funding for gross departures from federal program guidelines, made news when they occurred, and did bring about program changes. Similarly, when the Nader evaluation of the national CMHC program itself made news, it appears that Congress attended to the report and ultimately mandated changes in the program. We tentatively conclude that, in the final analysis, the relative advantages of internal or external evaluations depend heavily on the relative power of the program managers and the "outside" groups to use the results to shape the programs.

Program Improvement Versus Accountability. Since the late 1970s there has been a fairly strong shift from a program improvement or program advocacy focus in mental health evaluation activities toward accountability, cost cutting, and efficiency. A major contributor to this trend was James Sorensen, whose work (for example, see Sorensen and Phipps, 1975) provided CMHCs with sophisticated accounting and accountability tools to make this shift possible. The pervasive nature of this shift is apparent from the CMHC survey work of Larsen and Jerrell (1986). It is difficult to argue that this shift is inappropriate, since it fits the national political and financial climate of social conservatism that has emerged. Along with it, the internal administrative climate of many service programs has shifted from one of clinical concern over clients to one of sheer survival.

Still, we urge evaluators to preserve some formative, program improvement evaluation along with the more summative, accountability evaluation. The relative low level of understanding of mental health services clearly calls for expanding knowledge about services administration and delivery—which services work, in what ways and at what costs, to benefit clients.

Some Special Methodological Developments in Mental Health Evaluation

Although much mental health evaluation technology arose within the sociopolitical and program contexts described earlier, in response to specific needs of these programs (such as methods for studying continuity of care), some methods developed in very different contexts, were borrowed from other intellectual arenas, or have spread well beyond their initial settings. We will review here only a few of the more important ones.

Community Needs Assessment: Direct and Indirect Studies. Although the CMHC program required communities and states to do needs assessments as prerequisites for obtaining certain types of CMHC grants, little new technology was developed. Both within and outside NIMH, however, a few persons began adapting large-scale demographic analysis techniques to mental health-related planning purposes. Relationships of service use rates with a large variety of social indicators were explored, with special attention given to the decennial census as a rich source of catchment area and state characteristics that might be related to the need for mental health services. In the mid-1970s, NIMH developed the Mental Health Demographic Profile System, comprised of systematic extracts from the census, and made it available to state-level planners. Other indirect sources of needs information, such as community forums and surveys of knowledgeable community informants, were also developed (see Bell, Nguyen, Warheit, and Buhl, 1978). It became apparent, however, that these indirect needs assessment techniques required validation against criteria other than services utilization rates, since the latter are strongly affected by the availability of services.

In the early 1980s, NIMH funded a large study in Colorado to validate these indirect techniques against a direct epidemiologic population survey. This study is testing half a dozen social indicator procedures for estimating need for mental health services, using results of the Diagnostic Interview Schedule, or DIS (Robins, Helzer, Croughan, and Ratcliff, 1981) and several other need measures as validating criteria (Ciarlo, Tweed, and Shern, 1986). Results have confirmed the worth of many of these procedures relative to the assumption of uniform rates of need across areas. This study can be expected to increase the use of social indicator-based needs assessments for planning and funding mental health services in different geographic areas, especially at the state level.

A key methodological development here was the creation and use of the DIS to study the prevalence of diagnosable disorders in the general population. Administered by lay people, in household settings, the DIS produces frequency counts for key disorders, such as schizophrenia, and major depressive disorder. Although agreement of the survey data with clinician judgment has been quite variable in several studies, results from use of this instrument are quite consistent across five different metropolitan study sites (for example, see Myers and others, 1984) and comparable to the disorder rates found in the Colorado statewide survey (Ciarlo, Tweed, and Shern, 1986).

Other needs assessment techniques, such as community forums, nominal group approaches, and the Delphi approach (Siegel, Attkisson, and Carson, 1978) seem not to have caught on. However, expert consensus groups are increasingly being used to help decide what services should be provided as part of a standard treatment package for specific problems (Mullen and Jacoby, 1985). Use of the indirect key informant technique (based on judgments of people presumed knowledgeable about local conditions) is also apparently declining in needs assessments; this decline may be because federal requirements for such assessments no longer exist, or because of the similar eclipse of requirements for community participation in CMHC services planning.

Service Process Evaluation. Service process assessment became a key CMHC evaluation activity because the CMHC program emphasized such processes as availability, accessibility, and continuity of care (Feldman and Windle, 1973). These process evaluations are relatively easy to conduct, because most of the needed information is often available from agencies' data systems; instituting and using such systems was the most commonly reported evaluation activity among CMHCs (Kirkhart and Morgan, 1986). Process evaluation has successfully survived the end of federal CMHC funding, and is now common at both state and local agency levels. Program managers now realize that information on how many and which people are given what types of services by whom at what cost is essential to good program management. NIMH has steadily helped to develop and publicize methods for establishing and using management information systems (for example, Chapman, 1976; Paton and D'huyvetter, 1980), and continues this thrust in its collaborative Mental Health Information Systems Improvement Project with the states (for example, see Patton and Leginski, 1983).

Client Outcome Evaluation. Some evaluation studies attempt to determine either the impact of a program taken as a whole on subsequent client clinical status and functioning, or the influence of specific treatment patterns on such outcomes. This is the evaluation criterion of output or performance discussed two decades ago by Suchman (1967) in what is often considered the first true evaluation text. The complexity of this type of study makes it a more suitable task for externally funded services researchers than for local evaluators, and even under the best of circumstances it is difficult to accomplish.

Much less has been accomplished in this area than in process evaluation. Client outcome measurement was left out of most CMHC legislation and regulations, primarily because existing technology was both weak and costly. At a 1979 NIMH conference on evaluation, the first author of this chapter (Ciarlo) supported this position, despite some enthusiasm of the conferees for including client outcome in the developing performance measurement system. Only a few years later, however, the importance of client outcome data to the newly developing state accountability focus persuaded Ciarlo to call for greater efforts to evaluate changes in client functioning as a result of treatment (Ciarlo, 1982). A few state legislatures have tried to force the issue, requiring inclusion of simple outcome-type measures (for example, the Global Assessment Scale) in routine recordkeeping by all public mental health programs. NIMH also funded a systematic comparison of different types of outcome measures to facilitate measure selection in client outcome studies, and to improve the capability of local and state agencies (as well as service researchers) to do high-quality outcome work (Ciarlo and others, 1986). Nevertheless, many evaluators, including the second author of this chapter (Windle), believe that acceptable outcome studies are still too expensive and difficult to warrant broad application, and therefore may not be as worthwhile as much simpler studies of client satisfaction with services (especially if these studies can be administered by consumer representatives). It should be noted that the support of system managers and clinicians is still not sufficient to sustain a serious commitment to outcome measurement. A recent issue of the *Community Mental Health Journal* contains fascinating accounts of progress with, and difficulties in implementing, client outcome measurement procedures in several states (Diamond and Beigel, 1984).

Cost-Outcome, Cost-Effectiveness Analyses. Although the outcome side of cost-outcome and cost-effectiveness studies is still largely out of reach of most local (and perhaps even state level) evaluators, it appears that much of the technology needed for the cost side of such studies is at hand, ready for application as soon as the outcome data can be reliably and validly obtained (for example, see Sorensen and Grove, 1978; Yates, 1987). Some serious problems remain in handling hard-to-assess and hard-to-allocate costs, such as the burden on families caused by seriously disturbed clients being kept at home instead of in a hospital. But because good outcome measurement is still very difficult and expensive, these studies will remain quite rare for the near future, being done only when specially funded. As a consequence, these studies (as well as the still more technically difficult cost-benefit studies, which try to convert assessed client outcomes into dollar figures) are unlikely to figure in decisions of program managers and policymakers for some time.

In the meantime, we should view the results of cost-oriented studies with caution, and possibly as more harmful than no studies at all (1) if they fail to assess the relevant outcomes well, or (2) if they allow selection or assignment biases to distort the similarity of clients in different treatment conditions, or (3) if they ignore expected improvement in untreated clients over time. If equal outcomes are assumed in cost-effectiveness studies, or outcomes are assessed so insensitively that they appear to be equal when they are not, lower-cost treatments may be considered justifiable and subsequently implemented, when in fact client benefits are being eroded. We urge evaluators to take this threat seriously, and to undertake or support only those cost-oriented analyses that are balanced by adequate outcome assessment.

Community and Environmental Impact Studies. Evaluators apparently have learned to be extremely modest about what mental health services can accomplish for the community as a whole. Changes in a community's overall statistical "social indicators" (such as reductions in suicide rates and school dropout rates) are seldom proposed as realistic program evaluation criteria. Direct effects of mental health interventions on the 2 percent of the population that receives care are quite modest— between ½ and 1 standard deviation better than control groups' changes (Smith, Glass, and Miller, 1980); hence, it is unwise to expect to detect changes in statistics collected on 100 percent of the population. This caution does not, of course, argue against looking for evidence of system change from large-scale interventions in specific settings—for example, decreased employee absentee rates in a firm instituting a wellness or antidrinking campaign.

Evaluability Assessment. Evaluability assessment (EA), developed by the Urban Institute (Wholey, 1979), is essentially a set of rules about organizing a program, so that it can be subjected to formal evaluation in terms of its objectives. EA includes specifying the internal logic of the program and its objectives, verifying that the program can achieve the objectives, and setting measurable criteria for the degree of success in meeting objectives. EA was developed in 1974 for use with the national CMHC program, and finally applied in 1979-1980. In 1974 the CMHC program did not satisfy the evaluability criteria for agreed-on measures of feasible objectives (Wholey, Nay, Scanlon, and Schmidt, 1975), and NIMH program managers were reluctant to go through the lengthy analysis required to implement it. The later application was more fruitful, largely because its advocate was at that time a high-level administrator of the program. A system of performance measures for a limited range of objectives was developed and implemented.

Unfortunately, the promise of EA for the CMHC program was not realized, since removal of that program from federal control in 1981 shelved the performance measurement system. A subsequent EA of the smaller NIMH Community Support Program was judged successful, however, and EA is now being considered for use in connection with the evaluation of the Robert Wood Johnson Foundation demonstration projects of the organization of services for the chronically mentally ill in several cities.

Coordination of Services. A newly emphasized topic in mental health evaluation is formal assessment of the coordination of a wide range of services for a given target population. Such coordination often involves the chronically mentally ill, who require multiple services in different locations when treated and maintained in the community. In the few studies of services coordination for this group that have reached the formal literature, the results were most often unfavorable; for example, the 1977 GAO report severely criticized CMHCs for an apparent lack of interest in this client group, and for failing to coordinate the provision of catchment-based services for clients being discharged to their catchments from state hospitals. Studies of other target groups were more positive, however, showing good coordination of particular CMHCs with agencies such as police departments and courts in demonstration projects (Community Mental Health Project, 1980).

More recently, evaluation interest has shifted to the structure of interorganization agreements and networks, away from the performance of individual staff in effecting the desired coordination. We discussed this shift briefly in the earlier section on evaluation within the context of the federal Community Support Program.

The Use of Evaluation in Decisions and Policy Making. Our final topic involves the use of evaluations, including those never published, those summarized as tables or statistics, and those presented verbally to program decision makers. We view mental health programs as deeply embedded in political and social contexts, which do not change quickly or easily. Although the first author (Ciarlo) once believed that a single evaluation study, well focused on a crucial program issue and well executed, could induce a positive change in a service program, this conception has seldom been reflected in reality (for example, see Bigelow and Ciarlo, 1979; Rossman, Hober, and Ciarlo, 1979). Yet desirable program changes *have* occurred in many agencies, and some seem to parallel the evaluative feedback that was provided at some earlier time, both in local programs and at higher bureaucratic echelons.

We do not yet understand all the factors that go into either cognitive or behavioral change (particularly in organizational settings), even though this area of information use was itself conceptualized and formal studies of knowledge transfer in mental health programs began at least two decades ago. In the large number of studies done in this area, some of the factors that have been found to operate in the use of evaluations for decision making are the sociopolitical context of the program, the characteristics of the question studied, the quality and features of the study itself, and the relationships between the evaluator and the decision maker, including relationships to intermediaries (see Human Interaction Research Institute, 1976). Also many specific techniques or approaches to conducting and communicating evaluations seem to improve the chances of their use by mental health decision makers, although many of these are perhaps more clinical hunches than empirically confirmed truths (for example, see Stevenson and Ciarlo, 1982; Cohen, 1977). Nonetheless, we would urge both novice and experienced evaluators to give as much attention to maximizing the chances of evaluation results being used by the intended audience as to planning the study's design and statistical analysis. Frustration at seeing one's work neglected or even misused in program administration is both expectable and understandable; what is not acceptable at this stage of development of the evaluation enterprise is naiveté that assumes the automatic, well-intentioned, and thoughtful consideration of one's evaluative efforts by those for whom the evaluation is intended.

What We Have Learned—Evolution of a Discipline

In the last section we draw some conclusions about mental health program evaluation from the overview presented and from the experiences and interactions we have shared with evaluation colleagues over the last two decades. We hope this summary will serve as a useful starting point for people just entering the field.

Limitations of the Technology. As may be true of most new technologies, our greatest learning has been about its *limitations*. Our increased sophistication includes several realizations:

1. Program evaluations are not automatically valued by potential users, even though the intentions of the evaluators were the best and the execution of the work was of high quality. Some potential users want only selective information with which to promote a program or gain a competitive advantage, and objective assessments are often not welcome to such users.

2. It is more difficult to make evaluations useful for improving programs than it is to generate valid information about program performance, because management decisions involve many other factors, such as staff attitudes, costs of change, and expected results of change attempts. More knowledge about and attention to increasing the utility of evaluations to program managers, funders, and the public are badly needed.

3. Many scientifically *ideal* approaches to evaluating programs are impractical, because of their burden on the program, costs, and required evaluator expertise. Use of client outcome as a criterion comes first to mind, followed closely by cost-effectiveness and community impact studies.

4. Program evaluation seems to be more valued as a *process* than for its findings and their implications. Managers may view the activity itself as prestigious (since it shares some of the "scientific" mystique), and as a defense against criticisms of the program—for example, "We have a study addressing that very problem under way right now."

5. Evaluation approaches need successive refinements. For example, several agencies found that multiple generations of performance measures were needed to develop an acceptable performance measurement system. The same is certainly true for needs assessment techniques and client outcome study procedures, where major efforts to increase their accuracy and reduce their limitations continue.

Improvements in the Technology. Of the many improvements in evaluation technology that have occurred, the following seem noteworthy:

1. The working base of most effective program evaluation is a management information system (MIS) comprehensive enough to include client, services, and cost data, and flexible enough to retrieve them in desired combinations. Special data collections and analyses are normally used only to supplement studies done using an MIS. Most public mental health agencies either now have or participate in such an MIS.

2. Evaluability assessment is a useful first step in evaluation of large, complex programs; its focus on objectives and their measurement

is important to direct evaluation activities toward issues relevant to program management.

3. A program's process goals and objectives can be assessed with "performance measures" that are designed to monitor specified program processes (for example, controlling the ratio of inpatient to outpatient services).

4. Although client outcomes studies are still very difficult to carry out well, advances in the reliability and validity of client assessment instruments have been and continue to be made. More and more MISs are capturing information on changes in client status over time, as treatment progresses. In-community follow-up of clients is now expected as part of the effort to show the duration of program effects.

Spreading Knowledge About Evaluation Technology. Although this assertion is perhaps more difficult to defend than the previous points made, we argue that both the advantages and the limitations of program evaluation are better appreciated by program managers and funders than they were twenty years ago. This improvement is due partly to the *necessity* for managers to respond to accountability demands that were nonexistent then. However, there is at least some recognition by key officials that objective data about programs are important to justify and improve the programs over the longer term.

In addition, it appears that a wider range of interested parties is now asking for evaluation information, from local agency program managers to state legislatures and the U.S. Congress. Each of these echelons wants evaluation data specific to its interests and decisions; hence, echelon-specific evaluations may increase.

Lessons Not Yet Learned. Both the arguments among evaluators and their behavior suggest that there is still insufficient recognition of the following two key issues.

1. Programs will benefit from *both* external and internal evaluation, since each has distinct advantages and disadvantages. External evaluations can provide greater objectivity in choosing which program characteristics to address, and can offer a more critical and challenging perspective on a program. Internal evaluations, however, address more specific issues of immediate relevance to managers and the decisions they face. The two types also reinforce each other, in that external evaluations often require data from internal studies, may spur programs' use of findings, and may stimulate internal evaluations.

2. Even though it may be well executed and provides guidance for a managerial decision, a single evaluation does not "settle" a program or service issue. *Replication* in both the original setting and across similar settings is as important to extending our knowledge via program evaluations as it is in more formal research.

Long before another twenty years have passed, we expect that these issues will have been resolved and replaced by others, and that the "balance sheet" for mental health program evaluation will contain substantially more assets, fewer liabilities, and a correspondingly larger net worth.

References

Aiken, L. H., Somers, S. A., and Shore, M. F. "Private Foundations in Health Affairs: A Case Study of the Development of a National Initiative for the Chronically Mentally Ill." *American Psychologist*, 1986, *41* (11), 1290–1295.

Attkisson, C. C., Hargreaves, W. A., Horowitz, M. J., and Sorensen, J. E. (eds.). *Evaluation of Human Service Programs*. New York: Academic Press, 1978.

Bell, R. A., Nguyen, T. D., Warheit, G. J., and Buhl, J. "Service Utilization, Social Indicator, and Citizen Survey Approaches to Human Service Needs Assessment." In C. C. Attkisson, W. A. Hargreaves, M. J. Horowitz, and J. E. Sorensen (eds.), *Evaluation of Human Service Programs*. New York: Academic Press, 1978.

Bigelow, D. A., and Ciarlo, J. A. "The Impact of Therapeutic Effectiveness Data on Community Mental Health Center Management." In H. C. Schulberg and F. Baker (eds.), *Program Evaluation in the Health Fields*. Vol. 2. New York: Human Sciences Press, 1979.

Bradley, V. J., Allard, M. A., and Mulkern, V. *Citizen Evaluation in Practice*. National Institute of Mental Health, DHHS publication no. (ADM)84-1338. Washington, D.C.: U.S. Government Printing Office, 1984.

Chapman, R. L. *The Design of Management Information Systems for Mental Health Organizations*. Series C, no. 13. Washington, D.C.: National Institute of Mental Health, 1976.

Chu, F. B., and Trotter, S. *The Madness Establishment*. New York: Grossman, 1974.

Ciarlo, J. A. "Accountability Revisited: The Arrival of Client Outcome Evaluation." *Evaluation and Program Planning*, 1982, *5* (1), 31–36.

Ciarlo, J. A. "Evaluating the CMHC Program: Who Could Have Done It Best?" In W. Neigher, J. Ciarlo, C. Hoven, K. Kirkhart, G. Landsberg, E. Light, F. Newman, E. L. Struening, L. Williams, C. Windle, and J. R. Woy, "Evaluation in the Community Mental Health Centers Program: A Bold New Reproach?" *Evaluation and Program Planning*, 1983, *5*, 283–311.

Ciarlo, J. A., Brown, T. R., Edwards, D. W., Kiresuk, T. J., and Newman, F. L. *Assessing Mental Health Treatment Outcome Measurement Techniques*. National Institute Mental Health, Series FN no. 9, DHHS publication no. (ADM)86-1301. Washington, D.C.: U.S. Government Printing Office, 1986.

Ciarlo, J. A., Tweed, D. L., and Shern, D. L. "Validation of Social-Indicator Models for Estimating Need for Health and Mental Health Services." Presentation at American Public Health Association annual meeting, Las Vegas, Nevada, October 1986.

Cohen, L. "Factors Affecting the Utilizations of Mental Health Evaluation Research Findings." *Professional Psychology*, 1977, *8*, 526–534.

Community Mental Health Project. *Evaluation of Interactions Between the Community Mental Health Systems and the Judiciary*. Report of NIMH Contract no. 278-78-0066. Rockville, Md.: National Institute of Mental Health, 1980.

Cook, T. D., and Shadish, W. R. "Metaevaluation: An Assessment of the Congressionally Mandated Evaluation System for Community Mental Health Centers." In G. J. Stahler and W. R. Tash (eds.), *Innovative Approaches to Mental Health Evaluation*. New York: Academic Press, 1982.

Cook, T. D., and Shadish, W. R. "Program Evaluation: The Worldly Science." *Annual Review of Psychology*, 1986, *37*, 193-232.
Coursey, R. D., Specter, G. A., Murell, S. A., and Hunt, B. (eds.). *Program Evaluation for Mental Health: Methods, Strategies, and Participants*. New York: Grune & Stratton, 1977.
Diamond, H., and Beigel, A. "Introduction to This Special Issue on Statewide Outcome Evaluation." *Community Mental Health Journal*, 1984, *20* (1), 3.
Feldman, S., and Windle, C. "The NIMH Approach to Evaluating the Community Mental Health Centers Program." *Health Services Reports*, 1973, *88*, 174-180.
Flaherty, E. W., and Olsen, K. *An Assessment of the Utility of Federally Required Program Evaluation in Community Mental Health Centers*. Contract Report by the Philadelphia Health Management Corp. to the National Institute of Mental Health, NTIS PB-80207327 and PB-80207319. Springfield, Va.: National Technical Information Service, 1978.
Human Interaction Research Institute. *Putting Knowledge to Use: A Distillation of the Literature Regarding Knowledge Transfer and Change*. Rockville, Md.: National Institute of Mental Health, 1976.
Jacobs, J. H., and Thompson, J. W. "Lessons from NIMH's Operations Management System for CMHCs." In C. Windle, J. H. Jacobs, and P. S. Sherman (eds.), *Mental Health Program Performance Measurement*. National Institute of Mental Health, Series BN no. 7, DHHS publication no. (ADM)86-1441. Washington, D.C.: U.S. Government Printing Office, 1986.
Kirkhart, K. E. "In Support of CMHC Self-Evaluation." In W. Neigher, J. Ciarlo, C. Hoven, K. Kirkhart, G. Landsberg, E. Light, F. Newman, E. L. Struening, L. Williams, C. Windle, and J. R. Woy, "Evaluation in the Community Mental Health Centers Program: A Bold New Reproach?" *Evaluation and Program Planning*, 1983, *5*, 283-311.
Kirkhart, K. E., and Morgan, R. O. "Evaluation in Mental Health Centers: Assessing the Hierarchical Model." *Evaluation Review*, 1986, *10* (1), 127-141.
Larsen, J. K., and Jerrell, J. M. *Factors Affecting the Development of Mental Health Services*. Los Altos, Calif.: Cognos Associates, 1986.
Morrissey, J. P., Hall, R. H., and Lindsey, M. L. *Interorganizational Relations: A Sourcebook of Measures for Mental Health Programs*. National Institute of Mental Health, Series BN no. 2, DHHS publication no. (ADM)82-1187. Washington, D.C.: U.S. Government Printing Office, 1982.
Morrissey, J. P., Tausig, M., and Lindsey, M. L. *Network Analysis Methods of Mental Health Service System Research: A Comparison of Two Community Support Systems*. National Institute of Mental Health, Series BN no. 6, DHHS publication no. (ADM)85-1383. Washington, D.C.: U.S. Government Printing Office, 1985.
Mullen, F., and Jacoby, I. "The Town Meeting for Technology: The Maturation of Consensus Conferences." *Journal of the American Medical Association*, 1985, *254*, 1068-1072.
Myers, J. K., Weissman, M. M., Tischler, G. L., Holzer, C. E., Leaf, P. J., Orvaschel, H., Anthony, J. C., Boyd, J. H., Burke, J. D., Kramer, M., and Stoltzman, R. "Six-Month Prevalence of Psychiatric Disorders in Three Communities." *Archives of General Psychiatry*, 1984, *41* (10), 959-970.
Neigher, W., Ciarlo, J., Hoven, C., Kirkhart, K., Landsberg, G., Light, E., Newman, F., Struening, E. L., Williams, L., Windle, C., and Woy, J. R. "Evaluation in the Community Mental Health Centers Program: A Bold New Reproach?" *Evaluation and Program Planning*, 1983, *5*, 283-311.

Paton, J. A., and D'huyvetter, P. K. *Automated Management Information Systems for Mental Health Agencies: A Planning and Acquisition Guide.* National Institute of Mental Health, Series FN no. 1, DHHS publication no. 80-797. Washington, D.C.: U.S. Government Printing Office, 1980.

Patton, R. E., and Leginski, W. A. *The Design and Content of a National Mental Health Statistics System.* National Institute of Mental Health, Series FN no. 8, DHHS publication no. (ADM)83-1095. Rockville, Md.: National Institute of Mental Health, 1983.

Ray, W. A., Blazer, D. G., Scheffner, W., Federspiel, C. F., and Fink, R. "Reducing Long-Term Diazepam Prescribing in Office Practice: A Controlled Trial of Educational Visits." *Journal of the American Medical Association,* 1986, *256* (18), 2536-2539.

Rich, R. F. *Social Science Information and Public Policy Making: The Interaction Between Bureaucratic Politics and the Use of Survey Data.* San Francisco: Jossey-Bass, 1981.

Robins, L. N., Helzer, J. E., Croughan, J., and Ratcliff, K. S. "National Institute of Mental Health Diagnostic Interview Schedule: Its History, Characteristics, and Validity." *Archives of General Psychiatry,* 1981, *38,* 381-389.

Rossi, P. H. "Issues in the Evaluation of Human Services Delivery." *Evaluation Quarterly,* 1978, *2,* 573-599.

Rossman, B. B., Hober, D. I., and Ciarlo, J. A. "Awareness, Use, and Consequences of Evaluation Data in a Community Mental Health Center." *Community Mental Health Journal,* 1979, *15* (1), 7-16.

Scriven, M. S. "Evaluation Ideologies." In G. F. Madaus, M. S. Scriven, and D. L. Stufflebeam (eds.), *Evaluation Models: Viewpoints on Educational and Human Services Evaluation.* Boston: Kluwer-Nijhoff, 1983.

Siegel, K., and Doty, P. "'Advocacy Research' Versus 'Management Review': 'Nader's Raiders' and GAO on Community Mental Health Centers." *International Journal of Sociology,* 1978, *19,* 139-167.

Siegel, L. M., Attkisson, C. C., and Carson, L. G. "Need Identification and Program Planning in the Community Context." In C. C. Attkisson, W. A. Hargreaves, M. J. Horowitz, and J. E. Sorensen (eds.), *Evaluation of Human Service Programs.* New York: Academic Press, 1978.

Sinclair, C., and Frankel, M. "The Effect of Quality Assurance Activities on the Quality of Mental Health Services." *Quality Review Bulletin,* 1982, *8* (7), 7-15.

Smith, M. L., Glass, G. V., and Miller, T. I. *The Benefits of Psychotherapy.* Baltimore: Johns Hopkins University Press, 1980.

Sorensen, J. E., and Grove, H. D. "Using Cost-Outcome and Cost-Effectiveness Analyses for Improved Program Management and Accountability." In C. C. Attkisson, W. A., Hargreaves, M. J. Horowitz, and J. E. Sorensen (eds.), *Evaluation of Human Service Programs.* New York: Academic Press, 1978.

Sorensen, J. E., and Phipps, D. W. *Cost-Finding and Rate-Setting for Community Mental Health Centers.* National Institute of Mental Health, DHEW publication no. (ADM)76-291. Washington, D.C.: U.S. Government Printing Office, 1975.

Sorensen, J. E., Zelman, W., Hanbery, G. W., and Kucic, A. R. "Key Performance Indicators to Manage Mental Health Organizations." In C. Windle, J. H. Jacobs, and P. S. Sherman (eds.), *Mental Health Program Performance Measurement.* National Institute of Mental Health, Series BN no. 7, DHHS publication no. (ADM)86-1441. Washington, D.C.: U.S. Government Printing Office, 1986.

Stahler, G. J., and Tash, W. R. *Innovative Approaches to Mental Health Evaluation.* New York: Academic Press, 1982.

Stevenson, J. F., and Ciarlo, J. A. "Enhancing Utilization of Mental Health Evaluation at State and Local Levels." In G. J. Stahler and W. R. Tash (eds.), *Innovative Approaches to Mental Health Evaluation*. New York: Academic Press, 1982.

Suchman, E. A. *Evaluative Research: Principles and Practice in Public Service and Social Action Programs*. New York: Russell Sage Foundation, 1967.

U.S. General Accounting Office, Comptroller General of the United States. *Returning the Chronic Mentally Disabled to the Community: Congress Needs to Do More*. Publication no. HRD76-152. Washington, D.C.: U.S. Government Printing Office, 1977.

Weiss, C. H. "Research for Policy's Sake: The Enlightenment Function of Social Research." *Policy Analysis*, 1977, *3*, 531-545.

Werlin, S. H. *Assessing and Assuring Quality in Community Mental Health Centers*. Rockville, Md.: National Institute of Mental Health, 1976.

Wholey, J. S. *Evaluation: Promise and Performance*. Washington, D.C.: Urban Institute, 1979.

Wholey, J. S., Nay, J. N., Scanlon, J. W., and Schmidt, R. E. "Evaluation: When Is It Really Needed?" *Evaluation*, 1975, *2* (2), 89-93.

Windle, C. "Limited and Limiting Perspectives." In W. Neigher, J. Ciarlo, C. Hoven, K. Kirkhart, G. Landsberg, E. Light, F. Newman, E. L. Struening, L. Williams, C. Windle, and J. R. Woy, "Evaluation in the Community Mental Health Centers Program: A Bold New Reproach?" *Evaluation and Program Planning*, 1983, *5*, 283-311.

Windle, C., and Scully, D. "Community Mental Health Centers and the Decreasing Use of State Hospitals." *Community Mental Health Journal*, 1976, *12*, 239-243.

Woy, J. W., Lund, D. A., and Attkisson, C. C. "Quality Assurance in Human Service Program Evaluation." In C. C. Attkisson, W. A. Hargreaves, M. J. Horowitz, and J. E. Sorensen (eds.), *Evaluation of Human Service Programs*. New York: Academic Press, 1978.

Yates, B. "Cost-Effectiveness Analysis and Cost-Benefit Analysis: An Introduction." In D. S. Cordray and M. W. Lipsey (eds.), *Evaluation Studies Review Annual*. Vol. 11. Newbury Park, Calif.: Sage, 1987.

James A. Ciarlo is research professor of psychology and director of the Mental Health Systems Evaluation Project at the University of Denver. He co-edited the Community Mental Health Journal *from 1978 to 1981 and was a member of the President's Commission on Mental Health. He teaches, consults, and directs research in mental health needs assessment, program evaluation, and utilization of evaluation findings.*

Charles Windle is chief of the Mental Health Services Research Program in the division of biometry and applied sciences, National Institute of Mental Health. From 1969 to 1980 he conducted evaluations of the Federal Community Mental Health Centers Program and assisted local CMHCs to design and conduct useful self-evaluations. He now stimulates and monitors research grants on mental health services and the mental health service system.

Index

A

Abelson, R. P., 69, 80
Abt Associates, 30, 31
Achenbach, T. M., 78, 80
Adams, S., 92, 96
Administrative Agency Experiment (AAE), 30, 38
Aid to Families with Dependent Children (AFDC), 7-23; and AFDC-U 12, 13, 15, 18, 19
Aiken, L. H., 103, 117
Allard, M. A., 106, 117
American Evaluation Association, 1
Anthony, J. C., 118
Antisocial and Violent Behavior Branch, 67
Arizona: housing assistance program in, 30, 32-33, 34, 44; work-welfare program in, 7n
Arkansas, work-welfare program in, 7n, 11, 12, 13, 14, 16, 17n, 18, 19
Attkisson, C. C., 99, 102, 110, 117, 119, 120
Atwater, J. D., 73, 82
Audits, fair housing, 48-61
Auspos, P., 13, 25

B

Baker, S. H., 87-88, 96
Baldwin, D. V., 75, 78, 83
Ball, J., 13, 25, 26
Baltimore, work-welfare program in, 11, 13, 16, 17n
Bane, M. J., 14, 25
Beigel, A., 112, 118
Bell, R. A., 110, 117
Berck, P., 81
Berg, I., 88, 96
Berger, D. E., 79, 82
Berk, R. A., 86, 90, 92, 93, 96, 97
Berleman, W. C., 66, 80
Bigelow, D. A., 114, 117
Blakely, C. H., 81
Blazer, D. G., 119

Bloom, H. S., 1, 5, 85n
Bloom, S. P., 45
Bobo, L., 60, 62
Boruch, R. F., 77, 79, 80
Boston, racial discrimination in housing in, 52-53, 54, 56-57, 58, 60-61
Boyd, J. H., 118
Bradley, V. J., 106, 117
Bratt, R. G., 49, 52-53, 54n, 57n, 58, 60, 61
Braukman, C. J., 73, 80, 82, 83
Brown, E. D., 66, 73, 83, 97
Brown, T. R., 117
Budding, D. W., 43, 44
Buhl, J., 110, 117
Bureau of Labor Statistics, 34
Burke, J. D., 118
Byles, J. A., 87, 96

C

California: criminal sanctions in, 87, 88, 89, 90; work-welfare program in, 7n, 11, 12, 13, 15, 16, 17n, 18, 19, 21, 23, 24-25
Campbell, D. T., 96
Carson, L. G., 110, 119
Carter administration, 9-11
Cave, G., 26
Chamberlain, P., 73, 82
Chambers, D., 91, 96
Chapman, R. L., 111, 117
Chicago, work-welfare program in, 11
Child Behavior Checklist (CBC), 78
Chu, F. B., 102, 103, 106, 107, 117
Ciarlo, J. A., 3, 5, 99, 100, 105, 108, 110, 111, 114, 117, 118, 119, 120
Civil Rights Act of 1968, 47
Claude Worthington Benedum Foundation, 7n
Cobb, J. A., 78, 82
Cohen, J., 79, 80
Cohen, L., 114, 117
Cohen, P., 79, 81

Cohn, E. G., 95, 97
Colorado: citizen groups in, 106; mental health programs in, 100, 110; racial discrimination in housing in, 53, 54, 58
Community Mental Health Centers (CMHCs), 100, 101-103, 106, 107-109, 110-111, 113
Community Mental Health Project, 113, 117
Community Support Program, 103, 114
Community Treatment Program, 89
Community Work Experience Program (CWEP), 12, 14, 15
Conger, R. D., 78, 81
Congressional Budget Office, 11
Congressional Research Service, 7n
Consterdine, M., 96
Cook, T. D., 96, 105, 108, 117-118
Cordray, D. S., 1, 5, 79, 82
Coursey, R. D., 99, 118
Criminal sanctions: analysis of, 85-98; background on, 85-86; conclusion on, 95-96; deterrence by, 90-92; effects of, 86-95; interaction effects of, 92; lessons on, 2-3, 4, 86-92; no difference from, 86-88; recidivism increased by, 88-89; theoretical implications of, 92-95
Croughan, J., 110, 119
Cullen, F. T., 64, 65, 81

D

Dallas, racial discrimination in housing in, 53, 55, 56
Daniel, 85
Davidson, W. S., 69, 71, 72, 73, 76, 78, 79, 81
Delinquency. See Juvenile delinquency intervention
Demonstration of State Work-Welfare, 11-23
Dennis, M., 85n
Denver: citizen groups in, 106; racial discrimination in housing in, 53, 54, 58
Detroit: criminal sanctions in, 87; racial discrimination in housing in, 58-59
D'huyvetter, P. K., 111, 119

Diagnostic Interview Schedule, 110
Diamond, H., 112, 118
Discrimination. See Racial discrimination in housing
Dishion, T. J., 75, 78, 82, 83
Dixon, M. C., 65, 78, 83
Doi, D., 88, 89, 90, 92, 97
Doty, P., 108, 119
Driver Improvement Meetings, 90
Dunford, F. W., 75, 79, 81

E

Ecological Assessment of Child Behavior Problems (EACBP), 78
Edelbrock, C. S., 78, 80
Edwards, D. W., 117
Eggers, F. C., 48, 51, 52, 53, 54, 55, 57n, 58, 59, 60, 62
Elliot, D. S., 63, 75, 81
Ellwood, D. T., 14, 25
Empey, L. T., 88, 93, 96
Employment and Training (ET) Choices, 21
Emshoff, J. G., 81
Erickson, M., 25, 26
Erickson, M. L., 88, 96

F

Fair housing audit: design of, 48-50; lessons from, 52-61; and level of discrimination, 50; and probability of discrimination, 50-52; technique of, 48-52
Falkowski, C. L., 89, 96
Family Assistance Plan, 9
Family Interaction Coding System (FICS), 78
Farrington, D. P., 86, 87, 88, 96
Federal Judicial Center, 97
Federspiel, C. F., 119
Feins, J. D., 48, 49, 52-53, 54n, 57n, 58, 60, 61
Feldman, S., 101, 111, 118
Figlio, R. M., 75, 83, 94, 98
Fink, R., 119
Finkel, M., 31, 41n, 44
Fisher, R. A., 85, 97
Fixsen, D. L., 83
Flaherty, E. W., 102, 108, 118
Flanagan, T. J., 63, 81

Florida, work-welfare program in, 7n
Folkard, M. S., 87, 97
Ford Foundation, 7n, 25
Fort Logan Hospital, 100
Frankel, M., 102, 119
Freedman, S., 26
Friedlander, D., 13, 22, 24, 25-26
Friedman, J., 36, 39, 40, 44

G

Garrett, C. J., 67, 68, 71, 72, 81
Gartin, P. R., 88, 89, 90, 92, 97
Gendreau, P., 72, 81, 83
Gensheimer, L., 69, 71, 72, 81
Gerould, D., 25
Gilbert, K. E., 64, 65, 81
Glass, G. V., 67, 81, 83, 112, 119
Glick, B. D., 90, 98
Global Assessment Scale, 111
Goertzel, V., 88, 93, 97
Gold, M., 77, 83
Goldman, B., 13, 25, 26
Gomez, H., 77, 80
Gottfredson, G. D., 74, 81
Gottfredson, M. R., 63, 81
Gottschalk, R., 69, 71, 72, 81
Greater Avenues for Independence (GAIN), 21, 23
Green Bay Wisconsin, housing assistance program in, 30
Greenberg, D. F., 65, 81
Greenwood, P., 94, 97
Griffiths, D. S., 75, 81
Grove, H. D., 112, 119
Gruber, D., 26
Gueron, J. M., 1, 3, 4, 5, 7, 13, 15, 22, 25, 26, 27
Guy, C., 26

H

Hakken, J., 53, 57n, 62
Hall, R. H., 103, 118
Hamilton, E. E., 95, 97
Hamilton, G., 25, 26
Hamilton, R. A., 87, 97
Hamilton, W. L., 30, 38, 44
Hanbery, G. W., 103, 119
Hargreaves, W. A., 99, 117
Hawkins, G. J., 90, 94, 98
Hedges, L. V., 67, 81

Heintz, K. G., 31, 35, 36, 43, 45
Helzer, J. E., 110, 119
Herring, J., 81
Hindelang, M. J., 78, 81
Hirschi, T., 78, 81
Hober, D. I., 114, 119
Hoerz, G., 13, 25, 26
Holden, R. T., 87, 92, 97
Hollister, R., 49, 52-53, 54n, 57n, 58, 60, 61
Holshouser, W. L., 45, 49, 53, 54n, 55, 57n, 62
Holzer, C. E., 118
Horowitz, M. J., 99, 117
House, A. E., 78, 83
Housing. *See* Racial discrimination in housing
Housing Allowance Demand Experiment, 30, 32, 36, 37-38, 39, 40, 41, 43
Housing Allowance Supply Experiment, 30-31, 32, 37-38, 40, 43
Housing assistance programs: analysis of, 29-45; background on, 29-32; direct cash effects in, 36-40; issues of, 42-44; lessons on, 1-2, 3, 4, 31-32, 40-42; recent results of, 40-42; relative costs in, 32-36; studies of, 30-31
Housing audits, 48-61
Housing Voucher Demonstration, 31, 32, 40, 41, 42, 44
Hoven, C., 118
Huizinga, D., 63, 75, 81
Hullin, R., 88, 96
Human Interaction Research Institute, 114, 118
Human Resources Commissioners, 15
Hunt, B., 118
Hunter, J. E., 67, 82

I

Illinois, work-welfare program in, 7n, 11, 12
Indiana, housing assistance program in, 30
Internal Revenue Service, 91

J

Jackson, G. B., 67, 82
Jacobs, J. H., 103, 118

Jacoby, I., 110, 118
James, F. J., 53, 54n, 58, 62
Jerrell, J. M., 101, 109, 118
Jesness, C., 75, 81
Joint Commission on Accreditation of Hospitals (JCAH), 102
Juvenile delinquency intervention: analysis of, 63-84; background on, 63-65; and client characteristics, 72; conclusion on, 80; implementation of, 75-77; lessons on, 2, 3, 4, 67-73; optimistic view of, 65-66; and outcome measures, 72, 77-78; and rehabilitative ethic, 64; and research design, 72-73, 79; research framework for, 73-79; research on, 66-79; and statistical power, 78-79; targeting juveniles for, 74-75; and treatment efficacy, 67-73; and treatment integrity, 76; and treatment modality, 71-72, 76; and treatment strength, 76-77; and treatment theory, 74; and treatment variables, 72. *See also* Criminal sanctions

K

Kansas teaching family model, 73
Kaufman, P., 69, 70, 71, 72, 82
Kennedy, S. D., 1-2, 3, 4, 29, 30, 31, 37, 38, 39, 40, 41n, 43, 44-45
Kiresuk, T. J., 117
Kirigin, K. A., 73, 80, 82, 83
Kirkhart, K. E., 108, 111, 118
Klein, M. W., 89, 97
Knox, V., 25
Kramer, M., 118
Kucic, A. R., 103, 119
Kumar, T. K., 44

L

Labin, S., 89, 97
Ladd, H. F., 48, 62
Lamb, H. R., 88, 93, 97
Landsberg, G., 118
Langberg, N., 79, 83
Larsen, J. K., 101, 109, 118
Leaf, P. J., 118
Leginski, W. A., 111, 119
Lempert, R., 90, 91-92, 93, 94, 97
Lerman, P., 89, 92, 97

Library of Congress, 7n
Lichtman, C. M., 87, 97
Light, E., 118
Light, R. J., 1, 5
Lincoln, S. B., 89, 97
Lindsey, M. L., 108, 118
Lipsey, M. W., 2, 3, 4, 5, 63, 67, 69, 77, 79, 82, 84
Lipton, D., 64-65, 82
Loeber, R., 63, 75, 82
Long, D., 13, 22, 26
Los Angeles, criminal sanctions in, 88, 89
Lowry, I. S., 31, 38, 45
Lubeck, S. G., 88, 93, 96
Lund, D. A., 102, 120
Lundman, R. J., 65, 66, 82

M

McCummings, B. L., 53, 54n, 58, 62
McFarlane, P. T., 65, 82
McGaw, B., 67, 81
McGuire, R., 88, 96
McIntosh, N., 48, 62
MacMillan, J. E., 37, 38, 44
Maine, work-welfare program in, 7n, 11, 12
Manpower Demonstration Research Corporation (MDRC), 11, 12, 13, 14, 19, 20, 22, 23, 26
Mansfield, S., 32, 33, 34, 35, 36, 44, 45
Martin, S. E., 66, 82
Martinson, R., 64-65, 82
Maryland, work-welfare program in, 7n, 11, 12, 13, 14, 16, 17n, 18, 19
Massachusetts: racial discrimination in housing in, 52-53, 54, 56-57, 58, 60-61; work-welfare program in, 21
Maurice, A., 87, 96
Mayer, J., 69, 71, 72, 81
Mayo, S. K., 32, 33, 34, 35, 36, 44, 45
Memphis, criminal sanctions in, 87, 92
Mental Health Demographic Profile System, 110
Mental Health Information Systems Improvement Project, 111
Mental health programs: analysis of, 99-120; background on, 99-100; citizen/consumer study of, 102; community, 101-103; community impact studies of, 112-113; and

community needs assessment, 109-110; context of, 100-103; coordination of, 113-114; cost studies of, 112; decisions and policy making for, 114; evaluability assessment of, 113; external or internal evaluation of, 101-102, 107-109, 116; federal, 103; and goals evaluation, 107; and improvement or accountability, 109; lessons on, 3, 5, 114-117; metaissues in, 104-109, 116-117; methodologies for, 109-114; and outcomes studies, 111-112; peer review for quality assurance of, 102; performance measures of, 102-103; and research or evaluation, 104-105; roles in assessing, 105-107; self-evaluation of, 101; and service process evaluation, 110-111; state, 100-101; technology for, 115-116
Mental Health Systems Act of 1980 (PL 96-398), 101, 103
Merrill, S. R., 32, 39, 45
Michigan: criminal sanctions in, 87; racial discrimination in housing in, 58-59
Miler, S., 88, 89, 90, 92, 97
Miller, T. I., 67, 83, 112, 119
Minneapolis, criminal sanctions in, 86, 87, 90, 92, 93, 94, 95, 96
Mitchell, C. M., 81
Model Cities, 106
Morgan, R. O., 111, 118
Morrall, J. F., 33, 34, 45
Morrissey, J. P., 103, 118
Moss, W. B., 31, 35, 36, 43, 45
Mulkern, V., 106, 117
Mullen, F., 110, 118
Multifamily Development Cost Study, 31
Murell, S. A., 118
Murray, C., 65, 82
Myers, J. K., 110, 118

N

Nader, R., 102, 106, 107, 109
Nathan, R., 22, 26
National Academy of Sciences (NAS), 66, 67, 73, 74, 78, 79, 80
National Council of Community Mental Health Centers (NCCMHC), 103
National Institute of Justice, 87
National Institute of Mental Health (NIMH), 67, 100, 102, 103, 108, 109-110, 111, 113
National Youth Survey, 75
Nay, J. N., 113, 120
Nebuchadnezzar, 85
Neigher, W., 108, 118
New Jersey, work-welfare program in, 7n, 11, 12
New York: criminal sanctions in, 87-88; mental health program in, 100
Newberger, H., 52, 58, 59, 62
Newman, F. L., 117, 118
Nguyen, T. D., 110, 117
North Carolina, housing assistance program in, 34

O

Ohlin, L., 86, 88, 96
Olkin, I, 67, 81
Olsen, E. O., 33, 34, 45
Olsen, K., 102, 108, 118
Omnibus Budget Reconciliation Act of 1981 (OBRA), 11
Oregon Social Learning Center, 73, 74
Orleans, S., 90-91, 97
Orvaschel, H., 118
Osgood, D. W., 79, 81

P

Palmer, T. B., 89, 92, 97
Panel on Research on Rehabilitative Techniques, 66, 80
Parens patriae, in juvenile courts, 64
Paton, J. A., 111, 119
Patterson, G. R., 73, 74, 75, 78, 79, 82, 83
Patton, R. E., 111, 119
Pearce, D. M., 52, 58-59, 62
Pedone, C. I., 31, 35, 36, 43, 45
Pennsylvania. *See* Pittsburgh
Phillips, E. L., 83
Phillips, M. A., 76, 83
Phipps, D. W., 109, 119
Phoenix, housing assistance program in, 30, 32-33, 34, 44
Pittsburgh, housing assistance program in, 30, 32-33, 34, 44

Price, M., 13, 26
Program evaluation: of criminal sanctions, 85-98; of housing assistance programs, 29-45; of juvenile delinquency intervention, 63-84; lessons on, 3-5; of mental health programs, 99-120; of racial discrimination in housing, 47-62; of work-welfare programs, 7-27
Program for Better Jobs and Income, 11
Project on Social Welfare Policy and the American Future, 7n
Provo, Utah, criminal sanctions in, 88
Public Housing Authorities (PHAs), 29, 30, 31, 32, 33, 38, 43
Public Law 94-63, 101
Public Law 96-398, 101, 103
Public Service Employment (PSE), 10

Q

Quay, H. C., 66, 83
Quint, J., 13, 26

R

Racial discrimination in housing: analysis of, 47-62; audit technique for, 48-52; background on, 47-48; causes of, 59-61; conclusion on, 61; groups encountering, 55; lessons on, 2, 5, 52-61; level of, 50, 52-54; probability of, 50-52, 53-57; studies of, 52-53; varieties of, 55, 58-59
Rand Corporation, 30
Rapp, N., 81
Rappaport, J., 81
Ratcliff, K. S., 110, 119
Ray, R. S., 78, 82
Ray, W. A., 102, 119
Reagan administration, 9-11
Redner, R., 66, 76, 81, 82, 83
Reid, C. E., 48, 51, 52, 53, 54, 55, 57n, 58, 59, 60, 62
Reid, J. B., 73, 75, 78, 82, 83
Rhodes, W., 81
Riccio, J., 13, 26
Rich, R. F., 106, 119
Robert Wood Johnson Foundation, 113
Robins, L. N., 110, 119

Rockland, New York, mental health program in, 100
Romig, D., 65, 83
Rose, G., 87, 97
Rosenthal, R., 67, 69, 83
Ross, B., 72, 81
Ross, R. R., 72, 83
Rossi, P. H., 65, 78, 83, 105, 119
Rossman, B. B., 114, 119
Rubin, D. B., 69, 83
Russell Sage Foundation, 67

S

Sadd, S., 87-88, 96
San Diego, work-welfare program in, 11, 13, 15, 16, 17n, 18, 19, 23, 24-25
Sanctions. See Criminal sanctions
Scanlon, J. W., 113, 120
Scarpitti, F. R., 65, 66, 82
Schafer, R., 48, 62
Scheffner, W., 119
Schmidt, F. L., 67, 82
Schmidt, R. E., 113, 120
Schnare, A. B., 31, 35, 36, 43, 45
Schumaker, J. B., 83
Schuman, H., 60, 62
Schwartz, R. D., 90-91, 97
Scriven, M. S., 107, 119
Scully, D., 103, 120
Sechrest, L. B., 66, 73, 76, 82, 83, 97
Section 8: Existing Housing Program, 29, 31, 32, 34, 35, 40-41, 43-44; New Construction, 30, 31, 34, 35, 40-41, 43-44
Section 23, 30, 31, 32, 33, 44
Section 236, 30, 34, 35, 43
Seidman, E., 81
Sellin, T., 75, 83, 94, 98
Severy, L. J., 87, 97
Shadish, W. R., 105, 108, 117-118
Shaw, D. A., 78, 82
Sherman, L. W., 2-3, 4, 85, 86, 88, 89, 90, 92, 93, 95, 96, 97-98
Shern, D. L., 110, 117
Shore, M. F., 103, 117
Siegel, K., 108, 119
Siegel, L. M., 110, 119
Simonson, J. C., 48, 51, 52, 53, 54, 55, 57n, 58, 59, 60, 62
Simpson, G. E., 55, 62

Sinclair, C., 102, 119
Smith, D. D., 87, 97
Smith, D. F., 87, 97
Smith, D. J., 48, 62
Smith, M. L., 67, 81, 83, 112, 119
Smock, S. M., 87, 97
Social Interaction Scoring System (SISS), 78
Social Security Act of 1935, 8; 1967 amendments to, 9
Solnick, L., 25
Somers, S. A., 103, 117
Sorensen, J. E., 99, 103, 109, 112, 117, 119
South Bend, Indiana, housing assistance program in, 30
Specter, G. A., 118
Stahler, G. J., 99, 119
Stambaugh, E. E., II, 78, 83
States: mental health programs of, 100-101; work-welfare initiatives of, 11-23
Steed, C., 60, 62
Stegman, M. A., 34, 45
Stevenson, J. F., 114, 119, 120
Stoltzman, R., 118
Stouthamer-Loeber, M., 75, 82
Struening, E. L., 118
Suchman, E. A., 111, 120
Sumka, H. J., 34, 45
Supported Work, 21-22
System for Ecological Assessment of Child Behavior Problems (EACBP), 78

T

Tash, W. R., 99, 119
Tausig, M., 103, 118
Teilmann, K. S., 89, 97
Tennessee, criminal sanctions in, 87, 92
Texas, racial discimination in housing in, 53, 55, 56; work-welfare program in, 7n
Thompson, J. W., 103, 118
Tischler, G. L., 118
Trotter, S., 102, 103, 106, 107, 117
Tweed, D. L., 110, 117
Tynan, E. A., 53, 54n, 58, 62
Tyrer, S., 96

U

United Kingdom: criminal sanctions in, 87, 88; housing audits in, 48
U.S. Bureau of the Census, 34
U.S. Department of Health and Human Services, 101
U.S. Department of Housing and Urban Development (HUD), 29, 30, 33, 34, 43, 44, 45
U.S. General Accounting Office, (GAO), 101-102, 103, 107, 108, 113, 120
Urban Institute, 113
Urban Systems Research and Engineering, 31
Utah, criminal sanctions in, 88

V

van Alstyne, D., 68, 81
Venezia, P. S., 87, 98
Virginia, work-welfare program in, 7n, 11, 12, 13, 17, 18, 19

W

Wahler, R. R., 78, 83
Waldo, G. P., 77, 83
Wallace, J. E., 31, 34, 35n, 40, 41n, 45
Warheit, G. J., 110, 117
Warner, D., 32, 33, 34, 35, 36, 44, 45
Weichselbaum, H. F., 79, 81
Weinberg, D. H., 36, 39, 40, 44, 45
Weis, J. G., 78, 81
Weisbrod, G., 44
Weiss, C. H., 107, 120
Weissman, M. M., 118
Welfare. See Work-welfare programs
Werlin, S. H., 102, 120
West, S. G., 76, 83
West Virginia, work-welfare program in, 7n, 11, 12, 13, 15, 17, 18, 19, 20, 22
Whitaker, J. M., 87, 97
White, S. O., 66, 73, 83, 97
Wholey, J. S., 113, 120
Wienk, R. E., 48, 51, 52, 53, 54, 55, 57n, 58, 59, 60, 62
Wiley, B. P., 31, 35, 36, 43, 45
Wilks, J., 64-65, 82

Williams, J. R., 77, 83
Williams, L., 118
Willner, A. G., 83
Wilson, J. Q., 86, 88, 92, 96, 98
Windle, C., 3, 5, 99, 100, 101, 103, 108, 111, 117, 118, 120
Winthrop Rockefeller Foundation, 7n
Wisconsin, housing assistance program in, 30
Wolf, M. M., 73, 80, 82, 83
Wolfgang, M. E., 75, 83, 94, 98
Wolfhagen, C., 23, 25, 26
Work Incentive (WIN) Program, 9, 12, 13, 20, 21
Work-welfare programs: and AFDC reforms, 8-11; analysis of, 7-27; Community Work Experience Program in, 12, 14, 15; control group in, 15-17, 24; and evaluation research, 23-25; impact of, 14-19; interim findings from 13-19; issues of, 19-21; lessons on, 1, 3, 4, 19-21; and participation requirements, 13-14, 19, 22; policy impact for, 23; and Public Service Employment, 10; state initiatives in, 11-23; unanswered questions on, 21-23; workfare in, 10, 11, 12, 14, 15, 18, 20
Wortman, P. M., 79, 83
Wothke, W., 79, 80
Woy, J. R., 118
Woy, J. W., 102, 120
Wright, J. D., 65, 78, 83
Wright, W. E., 65, 78, 83

Y

Yates, B., 112, 120
Yeaton, W. H., 76, 79, 83
Yinger, J. M., 2, 5, 47, 48, 51, 52, 55, 59, 60, 61, 62

Z

Zeisel, H., 89, 98
Zelman, W., 103, 119
Zimring, F. E., 86, 90, 94, 98
Zwetchkenbaum, R., 32, 33, 34, 35, 36, 44, 45